IGNITE
YOUR
BUSINESS!

HOW TO LEAD YOUR BUSINESS TO GREATNESS

To Bill,

Wishing you every success!

Andrew

ANDREW SELLEY

IGNITE Your Business!
How to lead your business to greatness

Printed in the United Kingdom

Business
ISBN 978-1-5272-7320-7
Published by Terra Nova Business Services
Editorial Production: The Editor's Chair

About the Author

Andrew Selley has over 30 years of business experience, with more than 20 of them at board level. He is currently CEO of a 10-figure-turnover food company. He has turned unprofitable businesses into profitable ones, and doubled the profits of established businesses. He has worked in small start-up businesses and large global ones, in service-focused companies and with the world's biggest brands. He has worked in multiple business sectors and multiple geographies and cultures. In 2004, Andrew was named the Institute of Directors 'Young Director of the year' and was awarded the coveted Grocer Cup in the UK in 2019. His passion is to help leaders of other business exceed their goals.

To Kate, Aimée, Tasha and James

Acknowledgements

All of the amazing colleagues and managers that I have worked for and with at Bidfood, Bidcorp globally, and Coca-Cola Enterprises.

All of the people who encouraged me throughout the process of writing this book, especially Craig Ballantyne for making me put thoughts into action.

My Mum and Dad for introducing me to the *One Minute Manager* books, and the author Ken Blanchard for that series. These were the first business books I ever read and they inspired the 'Terra Nova' part of this book.

Denise Roberts and the editing and publishing team at The Editor's Chair.

The team from 'Black & White Coffee' at Bidfood, who inspired the café brand in the book and support educational projects in Tanzania through the sales of their coffee.

Anton and Elana Cuyler, who inspirationally set up and run SOZO, an education centre in Vrygrond township in Cape Town where they educate kids on studies and vocational training like barista, baker and hairdresser, and have their own coffee roastery.

The senior management team at Bidfood, who make business fun, engaging and successful.

Sir Clive Woodward, Sir Ian Cheshire and Craig Ballantyne for taking the time to read and comment on the book.

The Leicester boys, who will never cease to keep me grounded!

Recommendations

'I really enjoyed reading this book, especially the clear understanding of how success is driven by how you perform under pressure, which is a trait that can be learned and developed. Andrew's book will help you perform to your highest level. Insightful, practical and accessible—I have no doubt it will make you a winner.'

Sir Clive Woodward,

World Cup-winning Rugby Coach and Business Leader

'Whenever I find myself in a leadership or business growth struggle, I think "What would Andrew do?" Our conversations, and this book, have condensed 30 years of experience into powerful and practical advice for any entrepreneur, executive or leader that wants to grow their business and influence in life. Carry this with you everywhere.'

Craig Ballantyne,

Business Coach and Serial Entrepreneur

'Andrew Selley has used his extensive experience to write that rare thing—a practical business book. The clarity he offers is matched by a vivid storytelling approach to ensure the reader can then apply the insight for real. Read and learn and act!'

Sir Ian Cheshire,

Chairman of Barclays UK

Contents

Why Read this Book?

What's in it for me? Will I benefit if I follow your advice? What's it about, and how does it all fit together? Why should I listen to you?

Thank you for picking up this book. If you're reading this section to see whether you should buy the book, you probably have a lot of questions like the ones above! These are the questions I usually ask myself before buying a book. Time is precious—I don't like to waste mine and I'm guessing you're the same.

Let me help you decide whether you should buy this book by asking YOU a few questions. If you answer YES to any of the questions set out below, then I can guarantee that this book IS for you, and you will get instant, actionable content that you can use to improve your business:

Do you…

Want your business to be more successful?

Need quicker and greater results?

Wonder why some people succeed while others fail?

Want a formula that can guarantee your success?

Feel as though you're trying lots of different things that don't hang together in a coherent plan?

Feel like you're stuck in a rut at work and don't know how to get out?

Wish you knew the tips and tricks for business success?

Need advice from someone with a vast background of experience to help you in your current situation?

Worry that one day you will 'be found out' for your lack of experience and strategic thinking?

Want to find a 'fast track' and avoid the mistakes others have made before you?

Want a 'checklist' of things you can just go and try, and see what works?

And are you…

Looking for that extra edge, that one per cent all-round difference that will separate you from the competition?

Starting (or new to) a role that stretches you beyond your experience and need some assistance?

If you didn't answer YES to any of the questions above, then you're in a great place. In fact, you're probably a unique individual and should consider writing your own book! I've answered YES to most of these questions over the years (and still do to some of them).

If you did answer YES to some of the questions above, it's important to know that you're NORMAL. These are normal worries and fears and you're in the same position as millions of other business leaders. What makes you different is that you've decided to take action. You want to grow your knowledge, improve your skills and implement change.

As a leader you will probably always believe that your business is underperforming because you hold yourself to a higher standard, you never accept 'good enough' as good enough, and you are always looking for that extra edge. You can find that edge in this book.

This book is for you whether you're a CEO, a junior manager or a project team leader. Whether you have a thousand staff or three staff, whether you're a product company or a services company. This book will change your business and your life! That's a big claim, isn't it? If you're like me you would have heard it before and read books or listened to audio tapes, that promised to do this but failed to deliver.

So, why should you listen to me? Firstly, I've worked for over 30 years in business at the top level. I was the youngest sales director for the Coca-Cola bottling company in the UK when I was appointed. I worked my way up there from night shift manager in a warehouse within 10 years. I've run multi-billion-pound businesses in the UK. I've worked with start-ups as well as corporates, and I've also worked with not-for-profit and charitable organisations. I've worked at home and abroad. I've turned loss-making businesses into profitable ones, and I've taken an established multi-billion-pound business and transformed its performance, doubling the profits in five years!

Secondly, I've distilled all my learning and experience into this book. It's more effective than an MBA course (not to mention being cheaper, quicker and easier to understand!) and I can say that because I've done one!

I often have people seeking my advice on business, and the years I've spent in both large global and small local businesses give me a breadth and depth of knowledge to draw on that I've often taken for granted. The positive feedback and reactions from people I've advised, motivated me to translate this knowledge and insight into a simple but revealing and actionable book.

This is the book I would have wanted to read thirty years ago when I first started out in the business world. It's the summation of all the good aspects of business and success that I have learned over the years. However, I'm an imperfect human like us all. I've made mistakes, bad decisions, incorrect assumptions, and delivered bad results. These are all part of our life and our learning, and I've also incorporated this learning into the book.

Today, I have experience at senior levels in the world's leading product company and a global services company. As I've worked my way up in the world of business, I've learned something important from those I've met along the way. All of them have the same goal – to do the very best they can with the resources that they have, in the shortest amount of time and in the most efficient way possible. I believe you're no different.

If you're serious about business change – you can afford the time to read and absorb this book, and I know that it will assist you in step-changing your performance and reaching your goals.

Why IGNITE?

(Apart from the fact that it's a neat acronym?)

Without ignition there's nothing!

Ignition is the spark that starts everything. Without ignition, the car is stationary; with ignition, it can go to new speeds. Without ignition, the rocket is a statue; with ignition, it reaches new planets. Even with a new electric car – you need to flick the switch to get going!

Ignition – otherwise defined as 'agitation', 'disturbance', 'turmoil', and 'candescence'.

This book is about igniting your business. It's about just getting going, merely starting, and then exploding and delivering unbelievable change into your business, project, or team. I want to ignite the spark inside you. You have great ability and opportunity. No-one knows your business and your dreams better than you. You may have world-changing ideas or products swirling around in your mind. What I aim to do is to IGNITE those ideas and dreams. I'd like to help you give birth to your vision, harness your passion, and take your business and your team to the next level of performance.

I love a good bonfire! I love the power, the warmth, and the sense of community that's created around a big bonfire. I love staring into the everchanging shapes and colours of the flames and getting lost in my own thoughts. But without the spark, there's no bonfire. This book will help you IGNITE your spark and create your new reality—the power, strength, and community of your vision coming to life.

Or maybe your fire has died and the embers are barely smouldering. With good knowledge and action, that fire can be rekindled and burst back into flame. You have not failed until you give up. If this is your situation, this book can help you rekindle and reignite your flames.

Do you have unfulfilled dreams or repeated disappointments? Then IGNITE a new era, a new dimension of performance, and a new chapter in your life.

From that first spark that ignited our ancestors to discover fire, through the history of mankind, all great change and development started with a spark, an idea, a glimmer, that someone used to IGNITE their situation. **Ignition has always been the starting point.**

People are amazing. You are amazing. Your team is amazing. But most of us use only a small fraction of our amazing potential. The rest lies undiscovered and unstimulated. Ignite your passion for life and business, ignite your team's passion, and see how much more they can achieve. Ignite a force for change that can transform your life, your team's life, your business, your community and maybe the world?

Why I Wrote this Book

I've read too many business books to remember, many of them life-changing. Equally as many were instantly forgettable. I've often read management books that feel like a business lecture – lots of great theory, but I'm left scratching my head as to what it means in real life and how to action it. That's what compelled me to write this book. I did it to try to capture the best books' approaches – and avoid the pitfalls of the forgettable ones. Most of all I wrote this book to be USED and to be USEFUL. I wanted to give you ideas, examples and practical advice. I wrote it so you can read it and act upon it instantly, not read it and ask, 'What now?' I've experienced a huge amount of change, growth, success and mistakes in my business life and I believe that I have a skill in communicating and explaining things in a way that's actionable and relevant. This book aims to combine ideas with examples and action plans so you can instantly make a difference.

I wrote this book to build your confidence because most of the time it's a lack of confidence, or not knowing the right things to do, that cause businesses to fail. I believe that by giving you a structure and a plan that works for you and your situation, based upon years of top-level success and experience, you will not only avoid common mistakes but thrive in your success. However, I know that words, facts and wisdom without action is just information! The aim of this book is to enable you to take action immediately, big or small actions, long-term or short-term – it doesn't matter. What matters is starting! There are no detailed theories, no psychological 'mumbo jumbo', no patronising homilies, or superior gloating. All you will find is simple explanations of universal business principles and easy to follow actions. Business should be simple, straightforward, and fun – this book will help you in all these areas.

I wrote this book to challenge and channel your thinking and stimulate you to want to go further than you thought possible. I don't know your specific circumstances, but generally speaking, our circumstances are just the unique environment within which we operate. Fully understanding your environment (even though we have little control over it) is essential to creating the right actions. A valuable business 'formula' is:

$E + R = O$

E – Environment over which we have little control

R – Responses that we have to our environment, over which we have total control

O – Outcomes that occur as a result of our responses that feedback to the new environment

Environment + Responses = Outcomes

I want to challenge and channel your thinking on the responses that you will make in your specific environment, combining your unique knowledge with the ideas and actions offered in this book to create amazing outcomes.

How to Use this Book

This book will give you either a structure for a three-year plan, or a quick fix for an immediate problem – the choice is yours – use it how you wish.

You can work through the whole thing or dip into a chapter where you may be struggling in your business or with your team, and get quick, easy, and insightful analysis and a structured action plan in each area.

Each chapter is laid out in an easy-to-follow and accessible way:

- What does this element mean (e.g. Inspirational Vision)? What is the background to it? And, where does it fit into the overall business?

- Why is it important? What's in it for me if I do well in this area? Or, what will I miss out on if I don't do well?

- How do I achieve it? What are the steps to take and the areas to consider?

- Terra Nova Business Solutions parable (see below).

- Summary and next steps. Creating a plan that's easy to follow and unique to your business needs.

Terra Nova Business Solutions

At the end of each chapter, I develop an ongoing fictional story about a character called Bobbi and her work adventure at Terra Nova Business Solutions. Very often I've read books and can't visualise how the principles may apply, both positively and negatively, in real life. Throughout the book, I've used examples from my experience and the general business world to try to explain some points and also tried to help you see them in action at Terra Nova Business Solutions. The characters and situations are all based on my experiences in my working life and will give you a different way to access the content and guidance contained in each chapter. As stated above, this is fictional and any comparison to real-life people and businesses is coincidental.

With both real-life examples and 'business parables' from the fictional Terra Nova corporation, you'll discover how to transform your business, your project, or your team's day to day activities, and put them on the path to greatness. The key is to achieve great things with, and through, other people. It's to inspire and lead your team brilliantly, to influence others effectively in pursuit of your goals, and to establish a robust system that ensures you stay at the leading edge in your industry.

I hope you find the book useful and the format helpful. I'm always looking to improve as well as to engage with and help my readers, so please do let me know your thoughts and questions at andrew@igniteyourbusiness.biz

Okay, enough talking, let's buckle up and knuckle down… get ready to IGNITE Your Business!

CHAPTER 1

Inspirational Vision

* * * * *

'Begin with the end in mind.'
- Stephen Covey (author and educator)

* * * * *

'All men dream, but not equally. Those who dream by night in the dusty recesses of their minds, wake in the day to find it was vanity: but the dreamers of the day are dangerous men, for they may act on their dreams with open eyes to make them possible '
- T.E. Lawrence (aka Lawrence of Arabia,
British intelligence officer)

* * * * *

What is it?

What IS a Vision Statement? It seems a slightly ethereal concept, but the simplest and most effective way to explain it is that it's the 'true north' of your company. It's the 'end' that you have in mind at the beginning. It's the combined dreams and imagination of your business planted on the pinnacle, the mountain top that's always slightly out of reach. It's the aspiration that excites people, the aim that stirs people's imaginations and captures their hearts to make them try harder, go for longer, and aim higher than they thought possible. If you get it right, it's the game-changing element of your business. It's what creates your culture and separates you from the competition. It's the difference between success and failure!

I've heard it described as 'the finger that points towards the moon'. Your finger is not the moon, but the thing that guides and directs people towards the ultimate objective – and that's your vision.

Have you ever had that experience of being in a group – be it a sports team, a business, a community group, or a political group – where you all just 'got it'? You were all motivated, working together, putting in extra effort, celebrating successes, shrugging off setbacks, and racing to victory? It feels amazing, you're unbeatable and you're doing it for more than targets, objectives, or KPI's. You're doing it for how it makes you feel, because you believe in what you're doing because you love what you're doing. That's how it feels when you've bought into a team's vision.

You can employ great people, you can pay them and motivate them through performance bonuses, but you won't get truly exceptional performance unless you have a clear vision, and the team are bought into the vision. The vision is the flag that the team rally around. It must be true to your core beliefs and values, and also those of your team. That way, it can engage their hearts and minds.

Why is it important?

An inspirational vision is the key to building lasting success, and deep, real relationships at work and home. If you have a vision that captures your team's imagination, then your business will flourish. Suddenly, work will be fun, your team will be excited, it will be about US as a team, not you and them. You will all be looking to see how WE can move things on. You will all be asking, how can we move closer to this vision that we share? How can we help progress towards this vision that we care about? How can we push through setbacks to reach the greater goal?

With a shared vision, businesses work more efficiently, there are less politics and less territorial behaviour. The members understand what the team is trying to achieve, so are better placed to work together. The business is more efficient, nimbler, and more profitable than its competitors.

Without a vision that's bought into by all team members, then the opposite is true – work slows down, and initiatives are debated endlessly as everyone does not agree on the end objective. Politics rears its ugly head, departmental protectionism and budgetary games start to take place as people get distracted from the main aim of the business. There is no 'true north' against which to check the direction of travel so very soon the business goes off course. As much as an inspirational vision is vital, the absence of one can be fatal!

A vision statement should answer the deepest questions in the company:

- Why do we do what we do?
- Why do we care?

- What are we trying to achieve?

- What is our aim for the world?

- How do we want to make people feel?

- How do we want to be remembered?

When your team members are totally on board with your vision, they will go above and beyond the normal level of efforts to realise your vision.

* * * * *

'When you throw your heart over the fence, the rest will follow.'
– Norman Vincent Peale (American minister and author)

* * * * *

'It goes without saying that no company, large or small, can win, over the long run, without energised employees who believe in the mission and understand how to achieve it'.
– Jack Welch (CEO of General Electric 1981-2001)

* * * * *

People ask what the difference is between a vision statement and a mission statement. Put simply, a vision is the dreaming element – 'What do you want to change in the world?', whereas the mission is the doing element – 'What will you do? How will you do it? And who will you do it for?' A vision inspires, whereas a mission instructs. The vision is aspirational, whereas the mission is more practical. If you can't buy into the vision, the mission is irrelevant.

Your vision should be BIG, exciting and compelling. Almost impossible – but real enough to try to achieve. The vision should state what you hope to do someday, whereas the mission should state what the business should do every day.

Here are some examples of compelling visions:

'Our vision is a world without Alzheimer's.' – Alzheimer's Association.

'Our vision is to be earth's most customer-centric company, to build a place where people can come to find and discover anything they want to buy online.' – Amazon

'To make people happy.' – Disney

'To give people the power to share and make the world more open and connected.' – Facebook

'To organise the world's information and make it universally accessible and useful.' – Google

'To create a better every day for many people.' – IKEA

'To capture and share the world's moments.' – Instagram

'To bring inspiration and innovation to every athlete in the world, if you have a body, you're an athlete.' – Nike

'To be a company that inspires and fulfils your curiosity.' – Sony

'To accelerate the world's transition to sustainable energy.' – Tesla

How do I create an inspirational vision?

I cannot prescribe this as it has to come from your heart and the heart of the business. However, at the end of this chapter, in the Next Steps' section, I've laid out a framework for you to use with your team to have fun, be bold and create your own vision for your business.

This is the most personal element within your business. As business guru Simon Sinek would say, this should be your 'WHY?' – why you do what you do, what you stand for, the change you're going to bring to the world, the rallying call that will attract others with similar passions to work alongside you, and the motivation that will keep you and your team going through tough times.

Great leaders create compelling visions by carefully choosing words that connect personal meaning to a higher goal or purpose. This then creates a consensus of belief and a sense of direction for everyone in the business. Words have power – we can all think of a play, poem or song lyric that cuts us to the quick and makes our hair stand on end, no matter how often we hear it. Words connect with our soul and bring up our deepest feelings and energies. If you can get people's hearts, then you will have their minds and bodies.

Because your vision is unique to you, all I can do is point you in the right direction as I've done in the Next Steps section. The information provided will help you to create some structure and prompt some thinking techniques that will help you to IGNITE that spark and give birth to your vision.

Living out the vision

The biggest sin for a vision statement is to remain a poster on the wall or a screensaver. Visions must live, breathe and inspire, day after day. Think about when you go that extra mile for your family, or spouse, or church or charity – it's not because you get paid, it's not because you're logically calculating a payback, it's because you're 'ALL IN'. You're emotionally committed.

Your vision statement should narrow your company's purpose into a specific and powerful point of clarity, whilst at the same time give enough scope for innovation and diversity (in line with the vision), e.g. Tesla doesn't mention cars in their vision – but they do mention sustainable energy, so battery development and the innovations fit with the vision.

Your vision is the gatekeeper. Nothing should really get past it that doesn't take the business in the right direction. People who don't buy into the vision and values of the business should not be working for you. The easiest way to side-line the vision, as already mentioned, is to leave it as a poster on the wall or a screensaver on your laptop. It's amazing how quickly it can just become a piece of the furniture, rather than the living, breathing heart of the business. It's also very easy to see businesses that have abandoned their vision. Maybe *abandoned* is a little harsh – perhaps they just lost sight of it or ignored it for a bit. Your vision is the transparent standard against which all actions can be measured and it's very easy to see businesses that are out of alignment with theirs. It sticks out like a sore thumb and can be the beginning of the end for the business if not remedied. There will be plenty of advice and tips in later chapters on how to live out and embed your vision; it's well worth thinking up your own authentic ideas as well.

Your vision is the benchmark to hold ideas up against. At times, something – a project, plan, idea or even a person – may get past the gatekeeper level of your vision but when benchmarked against the high standards you aspire to it falls short. Your vision allows you to minimise the waste of time and resources on unimportant and distracting projects. Does something help fulfil your vision – Yes? Then go and do it. No? Then discard it.

Your vision helps customers, employees and shareholders know what they're part of, what they're buying into, why they should care and why you care. Very often now you see investment companies and investment funds actually looking at the vision, values and ethics of a business when considering their investments. 'Ethical investing' is an increasingly important part of the financial landscape and, hence, it's important for people to know your vision and values. In a similar way, many customer tenders, especially in the public sector, are interested in the technical compliance of a company with, for example, ethical trading and the modern slavery act, but also on a broader basis, they like to deal with companies who share their ways and values of doing business.

Your vision is the foundation of your business or venture. Ensure that your foundations are solid, ensure that they're true to your principles and values, and then ensure that the rest of the building is aligned with the foundations or else it will come tumbling down. With deep and solid foundations and true alignment, mankind has managed to build skyscrapers a kilometre tall. In business, if you get these things correct, then there is no limit to how high you can go!

The philosopher Nietzsche wrote, 'He who has a *why* to live for can bear almost any *how*.' In other words, if you create a compelling vision that your team and business can buy in to, and that's the foundation of your company, then your team can withstand many trials and tribulations, setbacks and problems because they believe in the WHY. They will understand changes in directions, changes in personnel and changes in products and services because they understand the WHY. If everything is moving in support of the vision, it's clear. If it isn't then it's just confusing.

Your vision can be unending (like making people happy or capturing life's moments) or it can be hugely aspirational and finite (like ending Alzheimer's). Finite ones are often described as 'moonshots', after President Kennedy's vision of landing a man on the moon and returning them safely. That's hugely aspirational and at the time seemed impossible, but obviously, it is still finite because after the Apollo 11 team landed back safely on earth, that vision was achieved.

Humans instinctively look to contribute to something greater than themselves. If you can provide that to your teams through the vision of the business then you'll see amazing loyalty, commitment and success. If you can't, then your team will seek that fulfilment outside of work, or in a different company altogether.

My own view is that either style is a legitimate vision for your business, but obviously, if it's a moonshot, you need to prepare for your next vision once you reach the moon!

Jon Kabat-Zinn, the renowned mindfulness practitioner, in his seminal book *Wherever You Go, There You Are*, told the tale of Buckminster Fuller, an American architect, inventor and futurist. He recounts how Fuller, before being recognised as a genius, had failed on so many projects he was contemplating suicide. However, instead, he decided to free himself and live 'as an employee of the universe' (to serve it rather than taking from it), devoting himself to the following question: ***What on this planet needs doing, that I'm uniquely equipped to do, that probably won't get done unless I do it?***

Now, that's a GREAT place to start with your vision! There's no danger of thinking too small or too narrow if you start by asking yourself that!

TERRA NOVA

BUSINESS SOLUTIONS

—— **OUR VISION** ——

Transforming the world through service solutions

——**OUR VALUES**——

Service, Trust, Integrity, Transparency

Terra Nova Business Solutions

Bobbi got out of her Uber and walked up to the sleek glass and steel frontage of Terra Nova Business Solutions' trendy offices in central London. She was incredibly excited. She couldn't believe her luck when she made it through the rigorous selection process as one of the new management trainees on the fast track development programme. She had spent ages getting ready and choosing just the right outfit – not too edgy, not too corporate, not too power-dressy, not too casual. Now, having told all her friends and family about her new role in this high-profile services business, she couldn't wait to get started.

The thing that she loved about the business (apart from the trendy office, free barista coffee and famous Friday night socials) was the company's vision and its values. She loved what they stood for and was excited to work for a company so focused on service and so embedded in their customers' businesses. She had seen clips of their CEO, Gavin, on YouTube, talking passionately about serving customers and tailoring their offering to individual customer needs. She was enthused with how he spoke and would have gladly worked there as an unpaid intern, never mind being on the fast track!

Etched in a smoked glass mural just to the left of the main entrance were the company's vision and values – proclaimed to the world like a royal coat of arms.

Our Vision: 'Transforming the world through service solutions.'

Our Values: Service, Trust, Integrity and Transparency.

Bobbi read these several times and felt a tingle of excitement – this is it, the big time. She took a deep breath and entered the sleek building.

Five minutes later she was still standing alone in the beautiful reception area. She had pressed the button that said, 'Press me in case of no-one being present in reception' but so far to no avail. She wondered where the receptionist was, and who it was that kept ringing out on the reception phone? Was she meant to pick it up in response to pressing the button? She decided not and pressed the button again.

After a few more minutes a young, well-dressed lady rushed in, hugely apologetic. 'Hi, I'm so sorry to keep you waiting. It's all a bit mad today. I hope you aren't put off. We're expecting you, Bobbi, and I was meant to be here to meet you so please accept my apologies. My name is Sue and I'm the director of people.'

Bobbi assured her it was fine. They went upstairs, via the nice barista coffee station, to Sue's office to go through her induction plan for the day, cover off the internal rules, health and safety, and associated admin. Bobbi knew that this was a necessary part of the induction but she actually wanted to get stuck into the business. She was relieved when Sue finished up and led her down the cool grey corridor to her first induction appointment.

'So, Terry is the purchasing director,' Sue explained. 'He is a bit of an acquired taste, but as long as he's had his coffee and a good night's sleep, he's usually fine,' she said with a smile and a wink. As they approached Terry's office Bobbi heard raised voices. Sue gently went to hold her back, but she was already entering the room.

There, a short, red-faced white-haired man wearing a rather-too-tight-across-the-stomach shirt was straining as he leaned across his desk towards a tall lady with striking short blonde hair and an equally red face.

'Maybe, I didn't make myself clear the first time,' growled Terry, clearly exasperated. 'I. Don't. Care. What. They. Want,' he said, accentuating every word. 'It's just too expensive.'

'Try actually thinking about the customer for once,' retorted the lady, standing her ground.

'One of us has to think about the bottom line,' shot back Terry. 'It's okay for you "fluffy folk" to be nice and cuddly to the customers but some of us actually have to make a living here!'

'You are impossible,' shouted the lady in response. 'It's always the same old story with you! You're the only one who knows how to make money, you're the only one who cares about the company's profits, blah blah blah!'

'That sounds about right,' Terry said smugly. At this point, the red-faced lady turned and brushed past Bobbi on her way out. 'This is not the end,' she said over her shoulder.

'Oh yes, it is,' Terry replied in a sing-song tone towards her departing figure.

Suddenly, Terry noticed Bobbi standing there, open-mouthed. He looked a little confused, and slightly embarrassed, but then looked at his desk diary and collected his composure. 'Ah, you must be Bobbi,' he said coming around the desk to shake her hand. 'Sorry you had to witness that – that's what happens when you have a passionate team.' He gave a 'what can you do' type of shrug. 'So, welcome to Terra Nova, what do you want to know?'

Bobbi was a little surprised by how quickly his temperament had changed. He was actually a normal colour now and didn't look like he was about to burst a blood vessel. She decided that caution was the best approach *with Terry until she got to know him better. 'I'm here on my first day of induction for the management trainee scheme,' she told him, 'and you're the first person on my list.' A little flattery never hurts, she thought!*

'Quite right too,' said Terry with a grin. 'I won't bore you with what we do and why we do it as I'm sure you'll get loads of that on your induction. The best thing I can do for you on your first day is to give you the same great advice my boss gave me when I started ten years ago.' He leaned forward over the desk as though he was about to tell her a secret. 'This is a good company and a decent place to work as long as you remember who you're working for! Don't let the customers run the place. That's why I was having that minor disagreement when you came in. Sales and marketing just pander to the customer – "Yes sir, no sir, how much sir, of course, sir",' he said in a mocking voice. 'In purchasing, we make all the money. Sales and marketing spend it! If we can ensure that they spend less than we make, then we will be successful, but it's a constant battle.'

'But I thought we were a service-focused company,' protested Bobbi, 'Aren't we here to serve and meet the customer's needs? Isn't SERVICE our number one value?'

'Well, you can't bank service and you can't pay people in values,' retorted Terry, 'although I admit that that IS the business we're in. It's just that some people take it too seriously, even to the detriment of profit – and we'll never be able to run a successful business like that.'

Bobbi spent another 45 minutes with Terry whilst he ran her through the structure and responsibilities of the purchasing department, but as she reflected on the experience later, she wasn't really listening to him. She was turning over in her mind what he'd said. What was going on here? She knew things weren't always perfect, but she was surprised to find such a dysfunctional team. And was service really a core value or did people just pretend it was? If so, how sustainable was that in the long run?

Next up on Bobbi's induction schedule was Penny, the sales and marketing director. Bobbi was unsurprised, as she approached the slightly ajar door to her office, to see that Penny was the lady who had been arguing with Terry. She knocked on the door but Penny didn't respond. She was staring into space as though deep in thought. Bobbi knocked a little harder with a loud clearing of her throat to get Penny's attention.

'Oh hi, I'm so sorry, I didn't see you,' gushed Penny. 'I'm Penny, in charge of sales and marketing.'

'Yes, I saw you an hour ago in Terry's office,' said Bobbi.

Penny blushed a colour that matched her pink suit and looked down. 'Oh no! I'm sorry you had to see one of mine and Terry's arguments! I'm afraid they're quite common. I suppose he's told you, 'I'm the one who makes the money and they're the ones that spend it'?' she said in a remarkably good impression of Terry.

Bobbi laughed, 'Something like that.'

'Well, he makes my life a bit of a misery that's for sure! In my area, we try to bring our vision and values to life, we try to sell great service to the customers, and we come up with some amazingly compelling offers. Unfortunately, we're sometimes restricted by finance and purchasing and end up having to dilute our customer offering, or even cancel initiatives we've already promised.'

'You can't bank service, Penny!' she said in another Terry impression. Bobbi laughed knowingly. Penny continued, 'I think his motto would be 'screw the customer' not 'serve the customer'! He's so short-sighted.'

'Why doesn't Gavin intervene and give some clarity?' Bobbi asked.

'Gavin is incentivised on annual profit improvement. So, unfortunately, he likes the money that Terry makes for him. It's quite frustrating, he talks a good game and I think he believes in the vision and values of the business, but he doesn't take a long-term view of service and returns. He just focuses on this year's numbers. Listen, I know we're a business, I know profit improvement is a key part of success, but we should be looking for service AND profit improvement, not one or the other. I get so sad seeing the vision, mission, and values getting sacrificed on the altar of short-term profit.'

Penny, who was staring out of the window as she spoke, suddenly snapped her focus back onto Bobbi. 'I'm so sorry, forgive me, I shouldn't be talking to you like this – it's not the best induction session you've ever had I'm sure.'

'If induction means understanding the truth about the business, then it's very helpful,' Bobbi assured her.

'I'm sorry, I just don't have anyone to offload to,' said Penny. 'Let's do a proper induction and let me tell you all about the department and our goals.' She pulled her chair alongside Bobbi's and opened her laptop to a prepared presentation.

As Bobbi walked to her last meeting for the day, with Phil, the operations director, she reflected on her meeting with Penny and again found that she hadn't really listened too much to her presentation either. Again, she had been processing what Penny had said before that. 'I really must concentrate better in my next meeting,' she thought to herself as she went downstairs to where the operations team were located.

Phil was a wiry, lean man who seemed to be constantly on the move – fidgeting, getting up, sitting down, stretching and scratching. This, combined with his spiky black hair, made Bobbi imagine that he was somehow connected to an electric current and was fully charged. She wondered if it was due to the stress of the job because after the introductions were out of the way, he also opened his heart to Bobbi on how things were for him.

'To be honest I feel like I'm the younger brother, stuck in the middle of a tug of war game between my older siblings!' Phil started. 'I feel like I'm pulled from pillar to post and back again. Promises made by sales are often undeliverable, as the budget agreed, or allowed, by finance and purchasing is not enough to deliver what was promised. We in operations have to try and deliver it, but then we also have to deal with all the complaints from the customers. It's all very stressful.'

Bobbi decided it was probably caffeine that was making him jumpy rather than electricity as he started on his second espresso of their meeting.

'It's a nightmare,' he continued, 'and to make matters worse if the customers get really angry with us, they often escalate the problem up to Gavin. He usually blames operations for messing it up and invariably agrees with the customer, and we have to fix the problem – which costs us twice as much as it would have done to just do it right in the first place. So we end up with an unhappy customer, high costs, a poor service experience, and a demotivated team – fantastic!'

Phil, like Penny, seemed to catch himself having gone too far. 'Listen, I'm sorry, I've just had a bad day. Don't worry about me, it's not that bad and I shouldn't be moaning to you on your first day anyway.'

'That's okay,' said Bobbi with a warm smile. 'I must have one of those faces people feel they can talk to.' Phil calmed down a little and for the next hour proceeded to take her through the overview of the department, its goals, and objectives.

After checking back in with Sue at the end of her first day, thankfully without too many searching questions on how she had found it, Bobbi stopped at the kitchen area to get a bottle of water from the fridge. She was approached by a timid looking man who seemed to pop up out of nowhere. She had seen him lurking around on a couple of occasions during the day.

'Hi, I'm Colin,' he said extending a limp hand to shake. 'I work in internal administration — otherwise translated as "everyone's dogsbody (and owner of all the company secrets)",' he whispered. 'How was your day?'

Bobbi gave him as little detail as she could, not naming names, but highlighting her surprise at the general lack of alignment of the process with the vision and values, and also the lack of 'joined-up' working between teams.

'Wow!' Colin exclaimed. 'You've sussed us out pretty quickly, haven't you?' He stepped closer and lowered his voice. 'It's a great place to work, once you know HOW it works if you get what I mean. It's not exactly as advertised but once you know who holds the real power you can usually navigate through the politics to get what you need. Just make sure you stay in Terry's good books,' he added over his shoulder as he scuttled off.

Bobbi put the water back in the fridge. 'I think I need a strong coffee actually,' she thought and texted her friend, Julie, to meet her at 'Black & White', the coffee shop around the corner. She had spotted it when she arrived and it looked busy, which was always a good sign.

The coffee shop was an oasis – amazing coffee aromas, beautiful casual wooden furniture, local art from schools on the walls, and the hubbub of happy customers. Bobbi ordered her hazelnut latte and a green tea for Julie and waited for her friend to arrive. She looked around at the seemingly happy staff. A young lady walking past her had a t-shirt saying, 'You're right – always!' on it. Just then Julie walked in and collapsed into the comfy sofa next to her. 'So, how was it?' Julie asked excitedly.

'Well, obviously I don't want to pass final judgement after only one day,' said Bobbi 'but I am pretty disappointed I'm afraid. I was so excited and so looking forward to working there. I love the stories, I love the vision and the values, and I love the way Gavin speaks with such passion about serving the customer.'

'So, what's the problem then?'

'It just feels completely misaligned and that, actually, half the team are more concerned about short-term profit than long-term success. I think what's most disappointing is that Gavin seems to swing between both points of view and doesn't provide the clear leadership through the business I was expecting – although I haven't actually spoken to him yet so it's a little unfair to comment – but that's how it feels.'

Bobbi took a long sip of her hazelnut latte then pulled a face. 'Wow, that's sweet!' she exclaimed under her breath. A passing server saw the expression on her face. 'Is everything alright madam? Anything I can help with?' he asked. 'Oh, it's fine, it's just a bit sweet,' Bobbi said. 'Maybe one too many syrup shots. It's no problem, I still like it.'

'That's no problem,' replied the smiling young man. 'You keep that, and I will get you a replacement made just the right way. My boss would be upset if he knew we had a disappointed customer.'

'Is he here now?' Bobbi asked. 'No, he only comes in once a week,' said the server, and then leaning forward in a pretend confidential whisper, he added, 'But he has re-enforced his values so often I swear it's like he has eyes on this place all the time.' Then off he went with a smile to get the replacement drink.

Bobbi turned to Julie with a mixture of delight and disappointment. 'Wow, look how great it is when all the team are on the same mission. The values of the business are understood, and lived up to by everyone, even when no-one else is looking!' She let out a long sigh. 'I guess today was only the first day at Terra Nova. Maybe it was an off day and things will be better. I probably don't understand things enough yet. In fact, I'm sure that things will get better.'

The server returned with her new drink and also gave her a half-completed loyalty card. 'We hope to see you back here really soon,' he said sincerely before hurrying off to clear some tables.

Terra Nova Review

Now review that situation and think about it in the context of your own business or team – what can you learn and apply, or change?

Specifically:

- *What are the three key reasons for Terra Nova not having alignment with its vision?*

- *What is the outcome in the workplace?*

- *Who is responsible?*

- *What specific actions would you suggest to Gavin that need to be done to improve the situation?*

- *Thinking of your own business – is there misalignment between your vision and your actions? What can you do TODAY to fix this?*

CHAPTER SUMMARY

An inspirational vision is the key to building lasting success with no limits. It's the secret to inspiring deep and real relationships at work and at home.

You need a vision that taps into people's passion and beliefs, that inspires others to achieve great things.

With a shared vision, businesses work more effectively. Everyone understands what is trying to be achieved, and they work together more effectively.

A vision statement should answer the deepest questions in a company:

- Why do we do what we do?

- Why do we care?

- What are we trying to achieve?

- How do we want to make people feel?

A vision statement is different from the mission statement. The vision is aspirational, whereas the mission is actionable. Simply put, the vision is the dreaming element, and the mission is the doing element.

Visions should be BIG, and they should be EXCITING! It's about answering the question, '***What on this planet needs doing, that I'm uniquely equipped to do, that probably won't get done unless I do it?***'

Having a vision statement is of no use unless the leadership team and the rest of the business consistently live it out.

NEXT STEPS

Let's write your inspirational vision! It may seem overwhelming to write it at first but you'll find it helpful to follow this simple structure to create and refine it.

A few tips to start with:

- Get your top team around you if you have one. The vision will be better-rounded with more input, and naturally, your team will believe it if they've helped to create it! This is so much better than presenting them with your finished version.

- Allow enough time to complete it thoroughly. Bearing in mind all I've said about your vision, it's not something to be dashed off in 30 minutes. Plan the time in and ensure everyone knows that this is what you're going to be doing. Preferably do it at the beginning of the day rather than the end when your creativity has been dulled.

- Think big! Actually, make your objective to have a creative and broad discussion of all aspects of the business and where it may go in the future. Hopefully, that will lead to your vision as well, or it may just lay the groundwork for another session. It's more important to get it *right,* rather than to get it ***done***!

- After you've completed it, take a week or two to sit with it and then get back together to ensure you're still happy with it. If not, tweak it where necessary. If it still doesn't feel right, then start again – you're going to be selling this vision for a long, long time – it has to be right.

- Finally, don't be modest! Your vision is the best, most exciting, inspirational version of yourself – so, don't hold back!

CREATING THE VISION

Step one

Think about the output of your company. Not necessarily what you do or create, but what the outcome of that work is.

For example, a cake shop may make cakes, but they could argue that the outcome is to bring joy and celebration to people's lives and taste buds. Or a coffee shop may make coffee, but they could aim to have the outcome of being the creative and environmental hub of the community.

Brainstorm the most audacious goals and outcomes your company could create; no idea is to be ridiculed or rejected at this stage. Re-read some of the visions at the beginning of this chapter. Notice that many of them are not about the product or service. Take the Disney example – 'to make people happy' – that's the output they're after. They don't mention movies or theme parks, they focus on the end outcome they aspire to achieve.

Don't analyse and criticise the ideas, just let them flow. Don't worry if your dreams are infinite or if it's a 'moonshot', just get them all on the table.

Step two

Consider what's unique about your company. What can only you offer? Or, what can you offer better than anyone else? Consider how this aligns with your company goals and values. Think about what you intend to offer in the future as well, not just what's within your current offering. Don't limit yourself into certain products, sectors, services or geographies. Dream about the future and be as broad as you can.

For example, your cake shop may want to only use organic ingredients sourced within 5 miles of the shop, or the coffee shop may aim to be the very first to use 100% recyclable cups, ensuring zero to landfill. They may want to only serve their local community, or they may want to go global.

Step three

Add some level of clarification on your target market. A vision should stretch the imagination but also provide certainty and clarity of direction. Are you targeting the entire global market for your product or service, or just national domination, or local domination of a variety of products?

For example, the cake shop could be everyone in the local region with something to celebrate, or if it has a great online presence, it could be the whole country. The coffee shop could be the whole community in a 5-mile radius, or if it has expansion aspirations it could join up communities to be the whole city, or all the cities in the country, or global domination.

You need to ensure that your uniqueness and your dreams are not misaligned. For example, it is hard to be global and commit to only sourcing products from a 5-mile radius, but the zero to landfill commitment is still possible.

Step four

Add some relatable, human, and real-world aspects. This is the 'Why are we doing this?' aspect. What will the world look like when we achieve our vision? Tap into your deepest feelings. Why are you doing this? What is motivating you? What do you hope to change in the world or your community? Envisage a time when everything has, or will, go to perfection. How does feel? What does it look like? Can you bring some of that emotional magic to life in your vision statement?

For example, the cake shop could aim to bring a smile every day to every person, or the coffee shop could be helping the community to feel like a family.

Bringing it all together

Visions are not prescriptive, and I can't give you a tick box checklist to complete that pops out your vision at the end. But if you follow the above steps and take your time, I know you will come up with something amazing. Be creative with it, have a laugh, but do some deep soul-searching as well. This is the purpose of your work-life after all!

For example:

Betty's Cake Shop: Bringing a smile to London, one cake at a time.

Black & White Coffee Shop: Bringing the community together, creating a family to save the earth.

CHAPTER 2

Galvanise into Action

* * * * *

**'You may never know what results will come from your action, but if you do nothing, there will be no results.'
- Mahatma Gandhi (Civil Rights Activist)**

* * * * *

What is it?

To GALVANISE means to impel, urge, motivate, excite, stimulate, invigorate, animate, energise, exhilarate and inspire. Does that sound exciting?

Imagine being in a business or environment where people were motivated, stimulated, animated, energised, exhilarated and inspired every day. Well, it may be a little exhausting if everyone was that wired every day, but you get the idea. Just thinking about that gets me excited. If all our teams were like that, we could surely change the world!

That's why this stage is so critical. As I've stated previously, *the BIGGEST threat to your vision and therefore your business is that it remains as just a poster on the wall.*

But that's what will happen unless you implement this stage of the process.

Why is it important?

How many times have you been in a situation where an initiative has been started but then just peters out, never to be revisited or mentioned again? I'm sure you have many times and know how frustrating it is. Even more frustrating is when it happens repeatedly – multiple new initiatives launched and not completed. This is why you need the energy and inspiration of galvanising people into action. If people aren't inspired, energised, motivated and animated about your vision then they won't do anything about it, and it will die. A lacklustre launch of an initiative, combined with underestimating how much action is required to see it through, are guaranteed to kill any idea.

If you and your team have spent time creating an exciting and inspiring vision, or a great new product or service, then why wouldn't you make the effort to launch and communicate it with equal excitement and passion? Remember, you've developed and created this initiative, discussed and brainstormed it, spent time getting excited and worked up by it. If, for your employees, it's the first they've heard of it – they haven't been involved, haven't bought in and haven't discussed it – you need to galvanise them into action. It's your job, and your duty, to inspire, motivate and energise them into action, and continuing action. This will be a combination of both galvanising the team and communicating effectively by following up to maximise the impact, which is covered in the 'Tell, Tell, Tell' chapter.

As it says in the Bible, 'Faith without action is dead' (James 2:26). Faith, belief, convictions, vision statements, mission statements and even *cutesie* marketing slogans, are all dead in the water without action, without someone actually getting off their backside and doing something.

I believe business is integral to and inseparable from life, so thinking about business situations through a 'personal' lens often helps to clarify things for me. I do this very often as it helps me see things clearly. People will say, 'You can't compare how you treat your employees with how you treat your friends and family' and if this is you then you're probably reading the wrong book! We need to be people of integrity and to act consistently whether it's in communicating with our kids or with our team. I believe that thinking like this will be an invaluable asset to you in the way you think about your business – with the same care and attention as you give your friends and family.

For example, imagine you were planning an amazing journey for your kids, the holiday of a lifetime. 'It will be amazing, children! We're flying first class to Disneyland, staying in the top hotel, and spending each day in the personal company of Mickey, Donald and Goofy. It will be the ultimate Disney experience: eating at all the themed restaurants, doing all of the rides, and actually riding in the procession.' Having painted this picture of the most amazing holiday ever, you then write down all the details for the kids so they don't forget and you put up posters around the house reminding them of the great trip coming up. You discuss it each Sunday over lunch and remind them how amazing it will be.

But then you do absolutely nothing! You don't book a flight or a hotel or a meal – zilch! Putting aside the fact that you should be arrested for child cruelty, how do you think your kids will feel when they realise that all you've done is talk about it and put a few posters up? Betrayed and disappointed. They probably will never trust you again and be suspicious of your future promises. I accept that may be a little excessive for kids who tend to have relatively short-term memories and easily forgive, but in the context of a business relationship, that's not unreasonable, I would suggest. Why should it be any different for your team?

If you've sold them an amazing vision, told them of the incredible possibilities ahead of the business and the wonderful future for you all, but then done nothing to deliver it – how do you think they'll feel? If you've publicised your vision with letters, posters and videos but done zero in terms of actions to bring it to fruition then your team will feel exactly the same as the let-down children in our example – betrayed, disappointed and mistrustful.

I also want to stress that now is not the time to get side-tracked by the delusion of perfection.

Voltaire, the French writer, said, 'The best is the enemy of the good.' Confucius said, 'Better a diamond with a flaw than a pebble without.' I've seen too many initiatives fail, or not even start, because people are seeking perfection rather than just getting going. You need to realise that there is no perfect plan. No matter how much time you spend planning and preparing, your plan will change and evolve as soon as you start implementing it, because no-one ever knows exactly what will happen in every circumstance. As the army saying goes – no plan ever survives the first encounter with the enemy! You obviously need to plan and consider different scenarios but don't get wrapped up in trying to perfect the minutiae of every situation. Get a basic plan and galvanise the team into action. We will look at perfecting after starting in a later chapter.

How do I do it?

So, it's important to galvanise the team into action – but how do you go about it? In my experience, it's best achieved by creating a sense of urgency. That sense of urgency is obtained by utilising one of the four methods below: time-related urgency, positive consequences, negative consequences or emotional urgency.

- Time-related urgency

This is usually the most obvious approach. We've often heard about the CEO's 'first 100 days' plan. All decent objectives and goals need to be time-related, so this makes sense. It's a simple way of ensuring everyone is focused (in other words, don't make the time frame too long!) and working together. Examples might be

- We need to hit £10m in sales in the next three months.
- We need to open 200 new accounts in the next 10 weeks.
- We need to collect all outstanding debts by the end of the month.
- We only have three months to save the business from bankruptcy.
- We need to exceed 95 per cent service levels for the next 12 weeks to save the business.

- Each salesman has to improve gross profit by 2 per cent in the next 12 weeks.

You get the picture. The more specific the better, and the task needs to be broken down into specific objectives. Break the £10m extra sales down by salesman or allocate the number of new accounts needed by each person. If you don't do that then people will not accept personal responsibility and it will remain a general aspiration.

Time-related urgency is a great way of galvanising action as it focuses people's minds on a goal and a timeframe. One word of warning though, which probably applies to all of these – don't overuse it! You can't create a crisis every other month and expect people to respond with the same level of energy. It's a great way to get things going and to create momentum, but it can't be your only motivational technique or else it will become just the normal way of doing things and lose all its effectiveness.

• Positive consequences

Always the preferable route if possible, it caters for the 'what's in it for me' approach. It could be a promotion for a limited number of people, it could be a bonus, it could be a team vacation, or it could be an extra day off. It can be whatever your creativity and budget can cater for. One of our warehouse managers introduced 'Thank Crunchie its Friday' and every week awarded a simple Crunchie chocolate bar to the most productive warehouse worker that week. A simple 50p chocolate bar had workers putting in massive efforts to be the winner. It wasn't the value of the sweet that made the difference, it was the recognition in front of their colleagues. Positive consequences don't have to cost the earth!

It's pretty simple really – we all like good things when they happen to us, and the promise of something tangible and good is a big motivator.

- Negative consequences

This is not as desirable as the option above, but sometimes the only option. When used sparingly, it can also be highly effective!

If we don't achieve this, we will lose our jobs! If we don't reach this level of income, we will all have to take a pay cut, etc. The consequences work a lot better when it's a 'we' approach – we're all in this together, rather than 'If we don't achieve this, YOU will lose your job!'

- Emotional urgency

This may be harder to achieve but if you can amalgamate the passion of the business with the vision and create long-term team engagement by galvanising them into action in a certain way, then this will enable great and long-term change. Emotional engagement is the 'secret sauce' that all great business leaders seek because you know the power of it and the change it makes, to you, your team and your business.

As the American poet Maya Angelou famously said, 'People will forget what you said, people will forget what you did, but people will never forget how you made them feel.'

A vision, as we have discussed, creates emotional buy-in and taps into deep feeling and values. This may, however, fade over time unless people are engaged emotionally on a longer-term basis. Keeping a team galvanised may be achieved by constantly communicating and reminding people of the vision and values to ensure that the fire doesn't die out. This is good and always a useful strategy anyway, but it doesn't DEEPEN the connection or commitment. It's like reminding your partner why you first fell in love with each other – always good to do, but it doesn't lead to a deeper connection.

My favourite method of creating engagement with the team or workforce is the 'You Said, We Did' approach. What's the easiest way to sell something to someone – give them exactly what they want! Why is it an easy sell? Because they have no objections and they're delighted to have found exactly what they need. 'Mr Jones, you said that you wanted a brown leather sofa for under $500 – here are several shades of brown leather sofas, of differing softness, for under $500.' I guarantee Mr Jones will buy something! 'Mrs Jones, you said you were only interested in this car in midnight olive, which is rare. I've found one for you at the budget you named – please sign here!'

If I tell you what I want, and you deliver what I ask for then I'm in! When we do that in business, in the workplace, then we create a new level of engagement. People often complain about being ignored or not listened to. By actively listening and ACTING upon what you're told then you will have commitment, galvanised employees, and emotional respect by the bucketful. The magic happens when you can meet the needs and wants of your employees and simultaneously fulfil the company vision – that's an unstoppable force.

In my company, we make a big thing of 'You Said, We Did' in most departments. We do it by taking all staff feedback from employee surveys and listening groups and acting on it, but more importantly, by telling and showing people that we have acted on it (detailed example below). Many areas will have posters up showing, 'You said you wanted X, we delivered X' or 'You asked us if you could have Y, you now have Y'. Very often when you speak to people and find out what they're looking to have improved at work, it's buried deep down, and they didn't even think about it explicitly until you asked them. Consequently, when you deliver against that desire it's often not noticed. Things seem better but they can't explain why – that's why 'You Said, We Did' is so powerful. When it's done consistently, there's a continual momentum of people feeling listened to and cared for, changes being made and action taken. That leads to gradual and consistent increases in action.

- Keeping the momentum

Galvanising people into action is not a one-time event. You can't rely on the enthusiasm and motivation to be long-lasting and keep going – in fact, you can almost guarantee it will need continual refreshing.

If you're deliberate and consistent in your efforts and if you continue to progress, then people will start to see that you're serious, and the levels of trust will increase. You may believe in what you say in your heart and reflect it in your plans, but your team will judge you on your actions. If they continually see you acting in alignment with what you say and what you're trying to achieve then they will start to believe and trust you more.

Once you can demonstrate progress and get increased levels of trust, you start to develop the 'evangelists'. These are the people who really buy into the vision and the direction that you're trying to go, and once they can see positive results, they get more excited, start to really engage, and push things forward in their own right. You need evangelists and you need others to help you. You can't carry the burden on your own, so you should consciously try to develop these in the team. Try to plan it so you get regular early wins, no matter how small – it shows you're succeeding. They say it takes five times as much force to get an object moving as it does to maintain its movement – that's the power of momentum! *Never underestimate how much effort you'll need to put in to start an initiative, but deliberately plan to create success and develop evangelists so you can keep the momentum going and progress accelerating.*

Example: 'You Said, We Did' – A case study from Bidfood UK

Bidfood is the UK's leading supplier of food and associated products to the UK hospitality industry (hotels, restaurants, schools, leisure venues, hospitals, etc). It's a company with $2 billion in sales and 5,000 employees. I took over as CEO in June 2014. It was perceived that the business was underperforming versus other similar businesses in the global group in other countries. Earnings Before Interest and Tax (EBIT) percentage was too low, and EBIT growth was too conservative. It's a company of long-serving employees where many senior managers have 15-20 years in the business (as do many people at all levels). I needed to create change quickly, and I needed the buy-in of the senior team. One aspect was creating an appetite for bigger, crazier growth targets. The other aspect was changing the culture of the business – which was perceived from the outside to be too complicated, stuffy, bureaucratic and slow-moving.

I wanted to create a mandate for change. I wanted everyone in the leadership to feel involved in the process, indeed I wanted them to BE involved in the process. I came up with a simple approach, which was quick, easy to do, highly effective and, most importantly, easily replicable in other situations.

I wrote to all of the senior managers in the business (about 150 people in total). I explained that I wanted their input, that I needed their involvement in the future style and direction of the business. I was looking for a quick and easy way to summarise the leaders' views and desires in the business, before planning what we did with that information. I asked them very simply for seven words: three words to describe how they thought the business was operating currently that they didn't like; three to describe how they would like the business to look and behave; and one word to summarise what they would like the business to be FAMOUS for. Seven words from 150 people – 1,050 pieces of information – not a huge amount of information, but gold dust in terms of the mood and feelings of the key players in the company.

I chased anyone who didn't respond because I wanted a hundred per cent response rate (an interesting insight as well regarding who might not want to participate in a direct request to shape the future of the business!). Once I'd collated all the answers, I spent some quality time with an Excel spreadsheet to make sense of them. I used some editorial licence, for example, when someone said that they wanted us to be innovative and another that they didn't want us to be traditional, as I believe they're saying the same thing. Similarly, if one said they want us to be 'premium' and another 'not the cheapest', then both are in the same camp. I was able to distil this information down to nine words that 90 per cent of the senior team said represented aspects of the current business that they would like to change, another nine words that 90 per cent of the business said represented the way they would like the business to look and behave, and one word that over 70 per cent of the senior team wanted the business to be FAMOUS for in the marketplace (this was the area with the most editorial licence – so if someone said we should be famous for service, another said quality, another excellence, another reliability – then I asked, can I find a word that encapsulates all these desires?)

The nine areas of behaviour that the senior team wanted to change were described as:

- Complex   -   Complacent
- Political   -   Reactive
- Rigid   -   Outdated
- Procrastinating   -   Disjointed
- Inconsistent

The nine areas of behaviour that the senior team wanted the business to emulate were described as:

- Dynamic   -   Flexible
- Visionary   -   Streamlined
- Dependable   -   Professional
- Passionate   -   Driven
- Aligned

The one thing that 75 per cent of the senior team wanted the business to be famous for was SERVICE EXCELLENCE!

With that very simple exercise, I'd created a mandate for change. Not only that but I had tapped into the start of the development of the company values. Albeit it was only the senior management team, which is about 2.5 per cent of the total workforce, but clearly an influential group. What they were telling me was that they wanted the business, and them, to act in certain ways:

- Be dependable, not inconsistent
- Be passionate, not complacent
- Be aligned, not disjointed
- Be streamlined, not outdated
- Be flexible, not rigid
- Be professional, not political
- Be dynamic, not procrastinating
- Be visionary, not complex
- Be driven, not reactive

From this launch point, I was able to galvanise a lot of action. I was able to restructure certain parts of the business (because the senior management team wanted to be more aligned and streamlined). I was able to both streamline and invest in IT (because the team wanted to be dynamic and visionary). I was able to set and agree on large increases in targets and objectives (because the team wanted to be dynamic, visionary and driven). We could invest in additional people and resources, as long as they were focused on delivering service excellence (because that's what the team wanted to be famous for!). But most of the benefit was derived because people bought into what we were trying to achieve as a business. They'd had their say, they felt listened to, they all had an element of the agreement, they could all see the direction we were aiming to travel in and, importantly, they all now had a common language. It was all about service excellence. We could evaluate all actions and projects – would it help improve service excellence? – if so then proceed, but if not, then rethink.

Terra Nova Business Solutions

Two months had passed since Bobbi had joined Terra Nova. In that time, she'd retained the thrill of coming to the exciting offices and had also reconciled herself slightly with the misalignment of values and actions. She convinced herself that this was not compromise, just a better understanding of the current business reality. She hoped in her heart that the values-driven approach would win out, but also accepted that Terry and the purchasing team did do a good job in making money so the company couldn't throw that away, could it? She also harboured a dream that she would progress through the organisation and get to a position where she could influence the playing field of results versus values – she wanted to have both. She could see Gavin's issue. How do you stick to your values when that means changing the department that drives the revenue? It's a big risk, she could see that, but then again, what's the ultimate cost of having a misaligned business? Surely to maximise the potential of the business you all had to be pulling in the same directions and using the same set of rules?

When pressed by Julie, she would admit to being slightly disappointed in the CEO, Gavin. He seemed rather weak and unable to kick the drug of profit at all costs and back some of the values-based initiatives – perhaps he was incorrectly incentivised, she mused to herself, or perhaps she was being too idealistic? 'Much to ponder,' she thought to herself.

In the two months, she had also become a bit of a regular fixture at the Black & White coffee shop. Thankfully, Julie worked close by as well so they met there regularly. Bobbi found it a real oasis in the city. There always seemed to be a genuine sense of togetherness with the team that worked there, and the customers, who seemed like old friends popping round for a drink. The attraction was helped by the fact that the young man who had helped her out the first time, who she now knew as Scott, had continued to be very helpful and friendly and – as Julie pointed out to her – was quite good looking! She often wondered if the business was as perfect as it looked. Did they have errant team members behind the scenes that disrupted the business but delivered good results? Did they only allow people to see what they wanted them to see, or were they genuinely aligned and working together on the same goals? Was it just like Terra Nova but better disguised?

This particular Monday was an exciting one for Bobbi. She had been asked to be part of a new project team – Project Genesis. It was a cross-functional team from different departments, different management grades, and different levels of experience. As she arrived in the room, with coffee in hand, she found that most of the other 20 people on the project were already there. They were obviously keen to get started as well – either that or they just wanted a good seat to watch the drama unfold, she thought.

The goal of Project Genesis was to try to identify and create new business streams for Terra Nova as there was concern amongst the board that some of the traditional business to business services may be declining. They wanted to seek new opportunities. Bobbi was delighted to be on the team. She saw it as an exciting challenge, and also an opportunity to grow her skills and share experiences with people from other areas. She knew about five of the people in the room already and they were well thought of, which reinforced her view that this was a great team to be a part of.

The only concern she had, and it was a big one, was that Gavin, in another sign of weakness (which he called inclusiveness), had appointed Penny and Terry as joint sponsors and co-leaders of the project group. This could be why everyone was there early so as 'not to miss any of the inevitable action'. There was an air of tension and anticipation in the room, with not too much idle chatter.

Penny and Terry arrived together – a show of unity – and Bobbi thought she was probably imagining the tight jawlines and slightly flushed faces on the pair of them! After five minutes of introducing themselves to the rest of the team, it felt to Bobbi like people were now settling back to 'watch the show'.

Terry, with mock servitude, doffed his imaginary cap to Penny and signalled to her to proceed. She started the internal sales pitch to the team:

'I want to say how delighted Terry and I are to be leading this project team. Make no mistake, each one of you was hand-selected to be in the group. We admire your abilities, experience, innovative thinking, and determination. We believe that we have the brightest minds in Terra Nova, here in this room to help us with this great opportunity.'

Bobbi and the rest of the group listened intently, and she felt that she was not the only one to sit up straighter, put her shoulders back, and glow a little with the opening praise.

'We've been given the opportunity in this team to create a rich and sustainable future for the Terra Nova business. Your creativity and commercial experience will be vital in helping us to discover, analyse, assess, and imagine the current as well as future demands of the marketplaces that

we operate in and could operate within in the future. This project and this team are being watched very closely by Gavin and the board and we're excited about what you'll deliver. Welcome on board and good luck to you all.'

'Wow,' thought Bobbi. A high profile, business-critical project that will secure the future of the business and that she had been hand-selected for – perhaps that promotion would be sooner than she thought, especially with the board of directors being so interested in the results. She hadn't noticed that Terry had now stood up until he cleared his throat to speak:

'I agree with Penny,' he said – and the look of surprise on everyone's face was a picture! 'This is indeed a great opportunity, but you also know what comes with a great opportunity – great responsibility and great accountability! I know some of you may struggle to get your heads out through the door after that build-up, but let's keep it real here. We're a business, successful but with tight margins. We want innovative ideas that don't cost much, that don't waste our time and money, and that don't take too long to deliver. Don't get carried away and tell us we need a unicorn when a donkey with a bit of glitter will do! Do you get what I'm saying? You HAVE been handpicked – but that's because we want results. If we don't get them quickly then we've probably picked the wrong team. Yes, the board is watching this closely, because this is key to the survival of the company, we need new income streams quickly to survive – if not then we will have problems. So, rest assured – Gavin IS watching – so watch out! Deliver quickly and you'll be heroes. Don't and you won't!'

They then went through some detailed roles, responsibilities, and timings and then the meeting broke up. Bobbi chatted to several of the team members who were as unclear as she was – was this a golden opportunity or a poison pill? Had they been chosen to succeed or chosen as a subtle workforce reduction plan if they were unsuccessful. They generally veered towards the line that Terry was right because as they all knew 'purchasing held the power'. Conversely, they also all agreed that Penny had made a compelling speech and motivated them to do their very best and see how it goes.

Bobbi sat in one of the trendy, coloured breakout areas and wondered to herself why it was all so confusing. Why couldn't everyone just work in the same way to the same goal? Was that too much to ask? Was it good to tell a team they were at risk if they didn't deliver? Shouldn't they have just motivated them and set them going, or was it better to be open and upfront from the beginning? Management and leadership were not as straightforward as she had thought when she was learning about them at business school!

It was definitely a Black & White coffee shop day, so she texted Julie to arrange to meet after work – she would need a strong one!

Bobbi almost felt herself relax when she walked in the store – it was an amazing feeling of buzzing convivial relaxation. She went for her usual hazelnut latte and green tea for Julie – well, she didn't actually as the server already knew what she wanted.

'The usual, Bobbi?' asked the quieter blonde-haired lady.

'Yes, please Gill, that would be great thanks.'

'No problem, would you like to try our special "Old School Roastery" beans, a little bit stronger and more rounded flavour – no extra charge.'

'Oh, yes please,' said Bobbi. 'When did that come in?'

'You haven't been in for a few days, have you?' Gill asked. 'You can read all about it on your table if you want – it's an amazing initiative.'

As she collected the drinks and walked over to the table, Bobbi could see Julie was already reading the leaflet that was on each table. She could also see posters up around the shop and all the waiting staff wearing 'Old School Roastery' t-shirts with 'Ask me about it!' on the back. As she put the drinks down, she saw Scott approaching. 'Scott – I'm not much of a reader and Julie's got the leaflet so as per your t-shirt, what can you tell me about the Old School Roastery?' Julie rolled her eyes at the subtlety of her friend, but Scott didn't notice. He was already animatedly into the download.

'It's an awesome new business initiative we launched this week. The owner has talked about it before, but at one of our monthly coffee club meetings – that's where all the managers get together with the owner to discuss the business – we brainstormed the concept and came up with a concrete plan. The owner has sold that plan so clearly into the business, with such passion, and the idea is so clearly aligned with our values as a business that it's gone down brilliantly and everyone is really promoting it.'

'Sounds great,' exclaimed Bobbi, slightly jealously thinking back to her experience that day. 'Tell me more.'

'In a nutshell, Old School Roastery is an initiative set up by the business, our own roastery. We offer vocational training in coffee roasting, barista, and service skills to young people who have been excluded from school. This way they get practical training to assist with getting a job or getting back into education. The coffee beans are sold on to the café, and also sold in retail outlets. Fifty per cent of the profits are donated to improve educational and afterschool provision in the local community.'

'Wow!' said Bobbi, genuinely impressed, 'And everyone seems keen to promote it too.'

'Yes,' said Scott. 'I think the fact that the original idea was the owner's but the team helped develop the detail really helped. Also, it's aligned with our values of service and community and we know that as well as making money we're doing good – that appeals to most of our employees.'

Bobbi and Julie chatted with Scott a bit longer and then debriefed each other on the latest gossip. On the way home, Bobbi couldn't help thinking again about the fundamental differences in her own employer and the little coffee shop team who were way more aligned, committed, and happy as a team than the people she worked with. 'Perhaps we should start to get Gavin to have his coffee there,' she thought mischievously. As she considered the different approaches, she thought that maybe the fundamental difference was in the context. Black & White had regular management meetings where ideas were discussed amongst the key players. The collective developed an idea which had then been nailed down into a firm plan, so they were already committed and motivated. Perhaps inspiration and integration are better than direction and implementation as a means of getting ideas transferred into reality?

Terra Nova Review

Now review that situation and think about it in the context of your own business or team – what can you learn and apply or change?

Specifically:

- *What galvanising tactics did Penny use?*
- *What galvanising tactics did Terry use?*
- *Which do you think is the better approach?*
- *What galvanising tactics did the owner of Black & White use?*
- *What are the benefits of this approach?*
- *What is your preferred approach and why?*
- *What can you do to try an alternative approach?*

CHAPTER SUMMARY

To galvanise is to impel, urge, motivate and energise your team or your business into urgent, immediate and ongoing action.

The biggest threat to your initiative becoming reality is not your competition, or the economy, or the political situation – it's you. Without you galvanising your team into action there's a danger that your dream will remain just a set of words or a poster on the wall. That's why action is so important.

Remember that the rest of the business is not as committed and emotionally invested in the vision as you are (this is less true if it's a small team and you were all involved in creating the vision, but especially true in medium or large businesses, or if you imposed the vision yourself). Because of this, you need to explain, engage and motivate them into action to help you achieve the goals – you need to galvanise them into action.

There are four main ways to galvanise your team:

- Time-related urgency – putting deadlines or timeframes by which a goal or target HAS to be achieved.

- Positive consequences – demonstrating and quantifying the positive benefits (financial, emotional, or social) that will occur when the goal is achieved.

- Negative consequences – demonstrating the negative impact (financial, social, or emotional) that will happen if the goals are not achieved.

- Emotional engagement – constantly communicating with the team on what you're trying to achieve, encouraging feedback, and generating debate. Try the 'You Said, We Did' approach of engaging your team and showing that you care about their feedback and act on it.

Remember:

'Imperfect action is way better than inaction.'

Case Study: The Bidfood Virtual Board

One initiative I used at Bidfood that worked well to galvanise our employees was to create a mini or virtual board team. Each board member selected a few of their team members who were young and talented (not necessarily their direct reports) and we asked them to work on new ideas for the business.

We had a briefing day, explaining why we'd selected them for the team and what we were expecting of them. We wanted effectively a full business review, SWOT analysis, PESTLE analysis, competitor analysis, that looked at all aspects of our current and future marketplace. We also tried to identify new ideas or initiatives we should be working on, current initiatives we should stop, and current initiatives we could expand.

The team worked over several months looking at all these areas, with regular review meetings with their board member. The end result was a day when the team presented back to the board on all the work they had done and the initiatives they proposed.

For commercial reasons, I won't go into the ideas here, but what they came up with had many direct and indirect benefits, as follows:

- The team were motivated, they felt great that they had been entrusted with such an important project.

- The team produced great ideas which we have used, or are using, to improve the business.

- The team developed its own cross-functional network. These are vital at all levels in a business. For someone in one area to have contacts in other areas that they can run ideas and problems by, is invaluable in developing a strong, diverse, and effective team.

- It helped the board to check whether their views on the calibre of the people involved were accurate and whether certain individuals over or underperformed versus expectations.

It's good to get new ideas, to motivate key individuals, create teams within teams, to take time out to coach, and develop the next stream of talent in a business. The virtual board team was a great way of doing all these things.

NEXT STEPS

Let's create a plan of action to galvanise your team and the others who you wish to influence, into action.

Step one

Map out all of the people you wish to influence and galvanise into action. This could be direct reports, indirect reports, the entire workforce, or other stakeholders such as customers, suppliers, or trade bodies.

Accepting that you want to influence all of them, prioritise the list so that the most important person to influence for the specific goal is at the top, and the least important is at the bottom.

Step two

The next stage is to articulate what type of outcome you're looking for from them. This could be active support (you want them to do something), passive support (you want them to understand and not oppose what you're doing), physical support (you want them to give you something or go somewhere), or financial support (you need them to give you money or funding).

Step three

Identify what action you'll need to take to achieve the biggest effect on each group or person, looking back at the type of motivators you could use.

Step four

Look at all the actions you've come up with. See if you can amalgamate them in any area. Prioritise them based on the prioritisation you have already applied in the importance of getting the support. Finally, create an action plan, prioritised, and time-defined.

An example is shown in the table below.

Stakeholder	Priority	Outcome Needed	Action Type	Action	Priority
Sales Director	1	Active support – embrace and deliver new sales targets	Positive outcomes time-related – hit the sales by end of year and get a bonus	Set targets, create motivational bonus, engage in vision and sell financial benefits	1
All Employees	1	Active support of the new targets for the next financial year	Emotional engagement and positive outcomes – Stress the importance of the targets and values, and how these will affect them. Stress the growth and opportunity that will come as we achieve the goals	Draw up a comprehensive communication plan (as per the Tell, Tell, Tell chapter) to ensure all the team are communicated to and listened to effectively	1

| Bank Manager | 2 | Financial support – finances to fund new CRM needed to support sales growth | Emotional engagement and positive outcomes – engage in vision and demonstrate financial benefits of increased sales and margin | Present financial plan of vision (i.e. impact of achieving it) to get emotional and financial buy-in. Monthly updates to keep enthused | 2 |
| Chairman | 3 | Passive support – buy into sales targets and potential outcomes (i.e. exit of sales director) | Emotional engagement | Sell the vision, and have monthly updates to communicate and keep engagement up | 3 |

CHAPTER 3

Nurture

* * * * *

'Trouble results when the speed of growth exceeds the speed of nurturing human resources. To use the analogy of growth rings on a tree, when unusually rapid growth occurs then the rings grow abnormally thick, then the tree trunk weakens and is easily broken.' - Akio Toyoda (President – Toyota Motor Corporation)

* * * * *

What is it?

To nurture means to care for and protect something while it is (or in the context of your team, they are) growing.

In the context of this book, we're talking about being able to care for and protect

- Your vision
- Your goals
- Your company
- Your team

When parents have a new baby, they don't bring it home, feed it a few times, and leave it – that would be absurd – but that's what many do with their new 'baby' of a dream, vision, or goal. When parents bring home a new baby, nurturing that child becomes their top priority. They reorganise their life and their schedules to provide maximum care and development. They have goals and dreams that they work towards and they allocate as much of their resources as they can afford to help in the child's development.

With your vision, project or product, would you just create it, show it off, do a bit of marketing, and then leave it and hope it grows, develops, matures, and prospers? No, because that's surely destined for failure. Can you see the absurdity of that situation? Yet we can all think of examples where that has actually happened.

Why is it important?

Nurture is the key to maturity and development. I don't want to be too simplistic, but without nurturing your children they will remain behavioural and intellectual babies. Nurturing is about managing that development process. Not too fast, not wanting to overload them, confuse them, overstretch them, expose them to things that are not suitable and so on. But also, not too slow, keeping them engaged, growing, stretched and developing them at the appropriate speed. Without all of this, your children don't fulfil their potential and similarly, without nurturing your business, or team, or vision, they too will not fulfil their true potential. We don't even have to think about it with the kids, but it's amazing how many business leaders completely forget or underestimate the importance of nurturing in the business context.

If you don't nurture your team, you are doomed to failure. It's as plain and simple as that! Failure to grow, failure to develop, failure to adapt or failure to achieve potential. That's not to say that the result is always an outright failure, but it certainly is always a relative failure in relation to what could have been achieved with proper development. There's also a lack of fulfilment on your part. Imagine a parent's disappointment who knows that they've let down their children, they haven't done all they could to give them the help and care they needed and, as a result, their children haven't been able to fulfil their potential. It could have a knock-on impact for generations. In our, say, fifty years of working life, we have only 438,000 hours to achieve all we want. Let us not fail due to lack of care and attention. Having a grand vision is of no use if you cannot nurture and develop it to fruition and beyond. If you don't, then it remains grand words and a waste of a dream. Nurturing ensures that fruit of some sort will always be born, and, ideally, a maximum harvest of greatness is achieved.

How do I do it?

This is a business book, not a parenting book, so I don't have to go into immense detail, but generally speaking, there are four ways that we nurture our children. Even if you don't have kids, I'm sure you will be able to relate to these examples pretty well!

Firstly, we nurture them by protecting them and enabling them to grow.

When we're looking at the world in a nurturing capacity, we look to see where danger and threat could come from for our children. We're aware of the dangers out in the world, we think about problems our children could encounter, we imagine the disasters that may befall them and how we can avoid them. We know the benefits of pre-emptive protection, such as vaccination, road safety, fire safety, 'stranger danger', and so on. We talk to them and remind them constantly of these dangers and how to avoid them. We never under-communicate, as any adolescent will tell you with a sigh: 'I know! Stop going on about it.'

We love our children and we want the very best for them. We want to give them all the chances we had or didn't have. We want to give them every advantage to succeed. We feel a similar 'love' for our vision, business and team (and if you don't have that emotional connection, then you need to go back to the start of the book as you have not correctly defined, or bought into, your dream).

We want to protect our vision or project, to give it a chance to become established and to grow. We don't want it to be suffocated by cynicism or apathy or to shrivel due to neglect. Think about what we said earlier about how we protect our children. We think and consider all the potential dangers, and we find pre-emptive ways of mitigating or stopping them from occurring. We tell our children over and over – we never assume it's sunk in. Our desire to protect them is stronger than our desire to not look stupid or risk offence.

We will want to protect our team or protect a project to ensure success (or at least prevent unjustified premature failure). We want our 'baby' to grow and flourish and reach all the potential we've dreamed of.

The one difference in protecting a vision or project as opposed to your actual children is to ensure that you *don't* do it defensively. If you're defensive or obstructive you will ultimately turn people against the idea.

As in the chapter on galvanising action, always try to give protection by stressing the positives, showing the upside, proving 'what's in it for them'. Emotional engagement and positive consequences are always preferable when you need to protect a vision.

So, think about the potential dangers and pitfalls that can befall your team or vision and make a plan to proactively protect them from these dangers. Try to think of scenarios and how you will react so that you're ready to defend your 'baby'. Thinking through scenarios will give you the best chance of proactive protection and also a range of options for when or if you come under a surprise attack.

Remember, if you can, to defend yourself and your vision with positivity and benefits rather than negativity and consequences.

In this way, your dream is more likely to survive and thrive throughout its 'early life' stages or sudden critical phases through to maturity.

Secondly, we nurture our children by training and educating them in academic, social, and emotional skills.

Whether we're teaching them to read, have good table manners, ride a bike, or do advanced mathematics, we would never bring children into the world and then just leave them as if they knew all they needed from day one.

Whilst you can't train and educate a dream or vision, you can educate the business *about* your vision, and you can educate and train your team to better *deliver* that vision.

If you're advocating fresh thinking, innovation, new processes, etc., then you'll need to educate and train those involved. You can never assume people will know what they're meant to be doing or how to do it, no matter how straightforward it may seem to you. We'll look at how we do the nurturing later in the chapter but remember that education and training do not need to be complicated. Often a lot of what's required is just good, clear communication. You bought the vision or business into being, you see the end goal, you need to take responsibility to ensure everyone is nurtured through training and education. The simplest way to do that, as we'll look at later in the book, is by clear communication. The old saying goes – never assume, it makes an ASS out of U and ME.

Never is that truer than in the area of communication, where we abbreviate and tailor our message based on what we THINK people already know. If you're going to assume anything, assume they know nothing and then you won't miss out anything important. Some say you have to repeat your message 10 times before people remember it, others say it is 20 times. I probably lean towards the latter number. The first few times you're just breaking through consciousness and all the other 'noise' in the workplace. The next few times people start to hear what you're saying and may start to question you on it. The next few times they're just listening to see if you're consistent – are they serious about this or is it just a fad? Finally, your message starts to be heard, believed, integrated AND acted upon.

A major error made by many people is to overestimate how much people know and understand, therefore underestimate how much they need to communicate and explain.

Imagine the scenario where the executive team have spent months with consultants developing their new vision, mission, and values. They've lived and breathed it during this time and now they're ready to inform the business. They put out a one-page brief on what the new vision is and why it's important. They stick posters up and put a copy of the brief on the staff noticeboard. Do you think people have bought into the vision? Do you think they have commitment? Do you think that vision is being nurtured, protected, and developed – no! It's dead on arrival – like a seed planted in the thinnest of soil it takes root but then dies. I've seen this happen and it's no surprise people don't get on board. They have no common level of understanding, as they all start with different knowledge levels; they have no emotional buy into the vision or values, as they weren't involved and no-one spends time explaining why they're important. Finally, people just wait for the vision, mission or values to die and disappear as they will if they're just written down and displayed.

I've seen scenarios where an amazing new idea or initiative is launched with great fanfare and razzmatazz. It's the flavour of the month for a few months, everything is linked to it and explained through it, but then just as quickly it disappears. A few months later a new initiative is launched and six months later another one. These are never believed or bought into as no-one sees any commitment from the top. Chopping and changing like that just stops people trusting that the latest initiative really is 'the one'.

Education, training, communication and explanation – keep doing it and never stop. As in the example of our nurturing parents, keep doing it even when people moan that they've heard it all before – as that may simply mean your message is starting to get through.

Thirdly, whether we would admit it or not, we nurture our children by trying to embed our culture and values into their minds.

We may deny it and we may say that we're raising them objectively to make their own choices, but fundamentally, unless we hate aspects of our lives, we'll do our best to 'pass on' who we are. If we're in a place where we like our lifestyle choices, our friends, our interests, and our beliefs, then we'll try to turn little Johnny into a United fan because we are. We get them into swimming or netball or rugby because we are. We take them to church because we go.

We chose our culture and values because we believe in them, we believe they're great, and we believe that they will be good for our kids. Some influencing we do deliberately – like taking them to United games. Other influencing we do almost without knowing because kids copy what they see. They copy our actions, mannerisms, and behaviour. They get their view of what is and isn't acceptable by looking at what we do and don't do. This is where you will get some interesting conversations with your children when your actions don't reflect your stated values or demands on your children – but we'll leave that one for the parenting book! Basically, if your actions are not in line with your values then you'll have an issue with your integrity (or perceived integrity).

Similarly, we devised our vision and goals for the business or team because we believe in them. We may have developed and communicated our values – again, not just to have the poster, but to have them as living, breathing, guidelines to the way we want the business to conduct itself. So, as part of the nurturing process, we want to immerse the business into the vision, values and culture.

Take every opportunity to reinforce these. Reiterate the vision in your internal communications, restate the values at the end of each social media post (#bestteam!), or word any announcements and press releases to encompass these things.

Most importantly, and as I will explain later, you need to **LIVE** the values and the vision.

Nothing will kill your vision and values quicker than inconsistent behaviour from the leader.

Imagine a leader trying to build a new culture of positivity and transparency, who just gossips and bad mouths people behind their backs – would you buy into that? Children tend to do what their parents do, not what they say – spookily, business tends to be the same!

In the chapter 'Tell, Tell, Tell', we'll look at different aspects of communicating and reinforcing your key messages.

Finally, we nurture our children by setting them free. We would do them no service to still be running around after them, cooking, and tidying up when they're 50 years old.

Gradually as they grow, we give them responsibility, autonomy and accountability until, ultimately, we believe we've nurtured them enough to let them leave and make their way in the world.

It's the same with your vision, goals, and team.

If you hold them close, do everything for them or related to them, never let anyone else get involved or don't release authority and accountability – they'll never grow, mature and have a life of their own.

Your team need to flourish with only a light touch of guidance; the whole company needs to be energised in delivering the vision.

You must have a target in mind to get to this stage, or else you'll be babysitting for your entire career. You need to have clear objectives for your team to achieve that means they're ready to move to the next stage of autonomy and responsibility. You then keep repeating that process. It's like the tricycle, then the bike with stabilisers, then Mum running alongside holding them up on the big bike, and then finally letting them go to freedom.

Keep setting the goals and keep progressing. Keep moving onto the next big idea, the next opportunity.

Protect them, train them, educate them, communicate with them, give them a cultural context, and develop them to the point where you can free them to go to the next level.

That's your point of success. That is nurturing.

Okay, you're probably saying, 'Please stop talking to me about my kids. I run a business and a team – give me some concrete examples that I can use at work to make a difference!'

Well, let's begin.

1. Be present

Primarily, similar to nurturing your children, the key point is to be present. Give your team your time, resources and attention, and when you do, don't dilute it by being distracted by something else. I'm sure, like me, you have been on the receiving end of being with someone who is continually distracted by their phone or their thoughts when you're trying to talk about an important business issue. How did that make you feel? Likely unimportant, belittled, irrelevant and so on. That's not how you want your team to feel. Similarly, like me, you may have come out of a meeting with your team or an individual and know that you have been the distracted one, whether it was an urgent call that pulled you away or something distracting you in your thoughts. You know you didn't give your team your best. I don't know about you, but whenever this happens, I always feel lousy. I know I've let people down and wasted their time. So, from both perspectives, find a way to remind yourself to be present, be in the moment and focus your efforts on your team.

Firstly, manage your time to nurture them effectively. Ensure you diarise time to nurture your idea and your team – assuming it's actually important to you (if it isn't, please return to the beginning of the book!).

Still, if we don't plan to succeed, we plan to fail, so make sure you diarise time. Time to work on your vision, time to review your progress, time to plan the next phases, time to work on your internal communications – basically just time to ensure your success!

Also, plan time with your team! You may see them every day, but you should still plan structured time to officially review progress against goals, give advice, mentor and also receive feedback from them. Keeping close to your team and the pulse of the business is vital to continued success.

2. Invest in the team

Manage your investment in the team to nurture them. If you want your team to be the best, be prepared to invest in their professional development or skills training. Training should be seen as an investment, not a cost. If you're training the right people, with the right skills, I guarantee you'll get your money back many times over.

When planning a big project, vision launch, or team development, it's vital to take a long-term view of investment and return. If you skimp at the beginning and expect to get something for nothing, you're very likely just to get nothing! Budget for investment in training, or communications conferences, or regular internal communications ideas to keep the vision intact and on track.

'But I can't afford it,' you say, 'we're a small start-up, we don't have huge budgets, and we have to watch every penny we spend.' That's okay, just be creative.

- Ask your team. There's a high chance that you will find someone who loves social media, videoing, editing etc., who would love to get involved practising and doing that at work.
- Utilise your contact network – find friends/contacts who could help with the job skills training or mentoring for your team. Who do you know who is good at marketing, negotiation, commercial analysis and so on? Can you get them involved?

People may not help if you ask them, but they definitely won't if you don't! Generally, I've found that people are willing to help and find it hard to turn down a polite direct request.

3. It depends on you – fully invest yourself

Be prepared to invest in nurturing emotionally and personally. It's your vision, dream, culture, team and company – you need to be *all in*.

You can't outsource your vision, your culture, your purpose.

People are intuitive – they know if you aren't fully invested – and if you're not, why the hell should they be?

People commit to things they believe in as we discussed earlier. They're persuaded by passion, they will buy into genuine belief, and follow true believers.

It's vital for your success that you commit fully and emotionally to proclaiming, feeding, leading and delivering your vision. Throwing money and time at your vision without putting emotional investment in is unlikely to deliver results. As I said, one of the biggest reasons for failure is a lack of trust in the leadership. Spotting misalignment between your words, your belief, and your actions will kill most things quickly.

Think of Steve Jobs at Apple, Elon Musk at Tesla, or Richard Branson at Virgin – you could never accuse them of not being all in – of not being totally passionate and invested in their brand. Yes, they sometimes get it wrong and show the downside of a larger than life association with the brand, but you can never doubt their commitment, and that motivates a lot of people.

Case Study: Bidfood – Repeat, Repeat, Repeat

We have three core values at Bidfood, developed by the team, lived and breathed in the business:

CARE – Take pride in what you do, no matter what you do.

SHARE – Work together to make great things happen.

DARE – Take brave steps to deliver extraordinary results.

In almost every communication I do, both internally and externally, where I know it will be read by our employees (e.g. trade press), I reiterate these values and weave them into the text. It continually reinforces that these are our values and we act in line with our values at all times. I've been doing that for years now and I know that everyone understands and believes in our values and our driven approach.

See the attached example where I was communicating to the wider business that we'd been awarded the contract to deliver food care packs for the government during the COVID-19 pandemic. This was an initiative we did in conjunction with our major competitor (Brakes).

Caring for the most vulnerable

Dear Colleague,

I'm proud to tell you that we have been awarded, in principle, the contract to deliver food parcels to the most vulnerable people forced to isolate completely in England.

Last Sunday the prime minister ordered 1.4 million people in England to stay in their homes for 3 months. These are people with serious health conditions who are most susceptible to COVID-19. The government has undertaken to ensure they get deliveries of food and medicines if they're not able to organise these themselves.

Last Thursday, on a call with the government about the likelihood of this happening, we DARED to do something different, and we came up with an idea that by working together with Brakes, we could put a system in place that would enable us to procure the product, pack the boxes, and deliver the food care packages to the homes of the people who needed them. It is unclear what the exact number will be who don't have support, but the estimation is 450,000. By SHARING this idea in conjunction with Brakes we can ensure that we have resilience and coverage across the country at all times.

It's a remarkable scenario where we end up working in partnership with our major competitor, but we're both driven by a desire to play our part in the national effort and CARE for those who need it most. I have to say that the teamwork demonstrated by both businesses has been humbling. The workload of packing the boxes will be spread across a few depots but the *deliveries will likely cover all the depots in England, depending on where the 1.4 million people are located.*

Due to the devolved nature of healthcare, our agreement only covers England, but we're already in discussions with the devolved governments to cover Scotland and Wales.

The volumes will not be massive at 220,000 deliveries a week, but it is a complex operation that we're not used to, and your site managers will explain how it affects your individual depots and departments. We still want to provide service excellence to our normal customers and our new home delivery and click & collect consumers.

I want to recognise the amazing efforts of many in buying, supply chain, finance and IT, as well as operations, who have worked all weekend to enable us to be in a position to start this ambitious project at such short notice.

It's an unbelievable time like none of us has ever known, and it has severely hurt the hospitality industry. Through our values, and our ability to react, respond, and innovate we're in a position to serve new customers and protect the most vulnerable in the country.

I want to thank you in advance for all of your efforts to deliver this over the coming weeks which I'm sure will not be without challenge, but I know you're the best team, and I'm excited to have the opportunity to show the country how amazing Bidfood people are.

Thanks,

Andrew

4. Release responsibility

Finally, there's the hard part of nurturing – extending responsibility and accountability up to the point of releasing them to freedom.

You can't run everything yourself, you can't run everything through you forever, and you can't keep everything in your control if you want to grow. If you're happy to stay small and not realise the breadth and depth of your potential, they maybe you can, but not if you want to achieve greatness.

Just as you nurture your children with the long-term (or medium-term, really) goal of equipping them with skills, training, and experiences to survive and thrive on their own in life – so too you want that for your vision or team.

You want your vision to survive without you – if it can't, then it certainly won't be a legacy for you as it will die with you. It has to outlast you. Similarly, you want your team to outgrow you. You should recruit people who can stand on your shoulders to achieve greater things and reach higher heights.

Great companies with great visions outlast their founders, just look at Disney, Walmart and Apple.

This is achieved by an absolute commitment to the vision and values of the business, and also by consciously creating an infrastructure to outlast the founder. Think of great leaders who have moved on or passed away and look at the way they prepared the business for that seismic event. Both Bill Gates at Microsoft and Steve Jobs at Apple recruited amazing people. They believed in recruiting people better than themselves, or with the potential to be so. The future growth and prosperity of the business were more important to them than their ego or standing in the business. They got great people, and they trained and nurtured them to be in alignment with the company vision and values so that this remained constant.

In the case of Microsoft, when Steve Ballmer took over as CEO from Bill Gates in 2000, he had already been in the business for 20 years and was fully aligned with the vision and values. He had already proven himself to be highly competent. When Tim Cook took over from Steve Jobs at Apple in 2011, he too had been in the business since 1998 and had fulfilled a variety of senior roles successfully.

Critically, the fortunes of both of these businesses have soared since the founding CEO was succeeded, which is a great testament to a remarkable job of nurturing and developing the team to succeed.

Notably, Apple had a market value of around $300 billion when Steve Cook took over and by 2019 was worth $1.1 trillion. Microsoft similarly went from a valuation of $200 billion when Steve Ballmer took over, to $900 billion in 2019. Undoubtedly, both are amazing examples of exceptionally well nurtured and developed teams.

Releasing your team is just like releasing the children. Sorry that it sounds so simple. I wish I could make it sound complicated, but most things in business are simple matters that people over-complicate.

You train your team, you set the guidelines, parameters and expectations, and you reinforce those with discipline and incentive.

Then, over time, you release elements of responsibility and accountability to them and see how they get on. If they thrive, you release more, if they fail, you circle the training loop again.

If they fail a few times, then this is one area where teams do differ from your children – you can consider changing the team member for someone more capable!

5. Don't have favourites!

Nobody should have a favourite child! You approve of the choices of one more than the others, or you may not like some of their actions sometimes, but deep down we love all our children equally.

It's really important as a leader to ensure equal authority, responsibility and status amongst your teams or departments. I've seen business organisational structures where IT reports into finance or HR reports into operations! That implies you don't value HR or IT as much. You need to identify the unique contribution each area makes and value and develop it fully. A coherent, fully aligned, cross-functional team will always do better than a siloed and divided team riven with interdepartmental politics. 'That's obvious', you may say, but many businesses set themselves up to create the latter kind of environment.

When I took over at Bidfood, whilst we were still developing the vision and values, I introduced the principle of UBUNTU. This is an African phrase that has been used by many (including Nelson Mandela during the rebuilding of the South African nation) that means *'I am because we are'*.

The story is told of a visitor to a poor African village who arrived bearing a massive basket of fresh juicy fruit. All the children of the village rushed to gather around him, clamouring for a piece of fruit. He told them all to go and stand by the tree at the other end of the village and said, 'When I shout go, you must run as fast as you can back to here, and the winner gets the fruit basket.' So the children went and lined up obediently. 'GO!' the man shouted. The children took off as fast as they could, big, small, young and old. By the time they were halfway through the race they were scattered out along the dirt track, some far ahead, others way behind. But then a remarkable thing happened. Those in front slowed down and those at the back caught up until eventually they all crossed the finish line together holding hands. They shared the fruit basket equally among them.

The visitor was intrigued and asked the strongest and quickest boy, who had been leading easily, why he had waited for the others. The boy looked at him quizzically and answered, 'How could I enjoy all this beautiful fruit on my own when I know that my brothers would go without?'

UBUNTU. We do it together. I am because we are. Unity. No departmental silos. No office politics. That was the message I preached whilst we were developing the vision and values to bring the company together as one team. I only talked about it for nine months, but six years later people still mention it to me. The power of language and longevity of good messaging!

Terra Nova Business Solutions

Bobbi felt energised as she got out of the Tube station on a surprisingly sunny morning. She was a bit worried that she'd noticed this, as it meant this was becoming the exception rather than the rule with work at the moment. She was enjoying being part of the Genesis project team and was learning a lot, but the divided leadership and guidance were draining and sometimes confusing.

As she walked towards the office, she saw Gill from the coffee shop and sped up to walk with her. They chatted amiably until they reached the coffee shop door.

'See you later, I'm sure,' said Gill with a smile.

'Without a doubt!' Bobbi replied.

She went into the Terra Nova offices so she could get ready for the reason that she felt energised today. Today was her monthly meeting with Sue, the HR director. When she had first joined, they had held the meeting every fortnight, but after three months they had agreed to move them to monthly. Bobbi did sometimes consider how she may have felt about work and the whole experience if she hadn't been having these meetings, but she shuddered at the thought and moved on.

She stopped off at the office coffee machine where she could now get a very acceptable latte (made with Old School Roastery beans that had been sold into the business). She saw Colin, the office gossip approaching. He had her in his sights, but she got away just in time, putting her phone to her ear as she walked back to her desk. Gossip and backstabbing were not the way she wanted to start her days.

As she sipped her latte at her desk, Bobbi reflected on why she looked forward to these meetings so much. Firstly, they made her feel valued. They were diarised in advance and were never moved or cancelled. They always started at 2 pm so there was no feeling of being rushed before, after, or during the meeting, and, at the risk of sounding vain, they were all about her! 'An hour or so a month to only talk about me, my issues, and my dreams is not much out of the 160+ hours available in the month,' she thought, 'but it's made such a difference to how engaged, valued, supported and motivated I feel.' She pondered on the difference that can be made by investing roughly 0.5 per cent of available time on an employee and the massive return on investment it represented.

Secondly, she liked the meetings because they were structured. There was an agenda, there was preparation from both sides, there was the space to share experience and also to share any problems. She enjoyed the way that the meetings allowed her to grow, both through advice and support, but also through challenges. These were not 'happy-clappy self-help' meetings. She was often challenged to justify statements or actions and sometimes felt quite uncomfortable but because it was in this meeting, which focused on her development, it always felt safe as well. They had used the meetings to develop training options and secondment ideas for her that specifically met her needs most effectively. Finally, she enjoyed the meetings as they allowed her to plan and dream, to talk about her aspirations and promotion goals and to identify what was realistic and what skills she may need to develop. Basically, she summarised to herself, 'It gets me motivated and engaged because it's all about investing in me, listening to me and valuing me as a person.'

It helped her that the meetings were with Sue. Firstly, Sue had assured her that what they discussed stayed between them, and Bobbi believed her.

Secondly, it was good that Bobbi didn't report directly to Sue, but she was a senior executive who understood what was going on in different areas. Bobbi felt able to be open with her and discuss things that she would not have been able to do so openly if it had been with her boss. She could say what she thought whereas sometimes with her boss she tempered what she wanted to say by thinking what he would WANT her to say. Being able to discuss things openly was not only more effective from an action planning point of view but also felt very liberating.

Bobbi finished up her prep for the meeting and then turned her attention to her task list for the day. 'Probably need another latte to power me through this lot,' she thought and went back over to the coffee machine area. As if by magic, Colin appeared from nowhere.

'Hi, Bobbi, how are you?'

'Fine thanks, Colin, quite busy actually.'

'Oh, I know, tell me about it! It's all a bit crazy over in the operations department. Did you hear about Phil's operational excellence launch?' Colin did the annoying quotation marks with his fingers as he said, 'operational excellence'.

Bobbi had been getting a bit worried about Phil. He always looked three espressos away from a breakdown, too busy, too little time, and too many conflicting demands on his team from Penny and Terry. He was tightly wound up at the best of times. He was always excellent at getting things done she thought, but only if he saw value in doing it. If he thought it was a waste of his time, he either tended to ignore it or did the bare minimum required, just so he could say he had done something.

Colin proceeded to tell her, with some relish it seemed to her, about Phil's attempt to launch an operational excellence initiative into the department. It seemed he wanted to launch it but couldn't spare the time. He'd created the plan during an away weekend with his senior team (which actually became an away 'Saturday morning' because a crisis had broken out in the facilities management area of the business to do with power supply and generators after contractors cut through the wrong cables). He then finished the plan himself and briefed it to the team one morning. He sent an email to those situated away from head office and backed it all up with special posters and a screensaver. Bobbi thought it sounded like one of those times when he hadn't seen the value in what he was doing. Instead of involving the team, he had briefed his direct reports on what he thought they should do and then had just sent an email (one of the worst ways to brief something important) to the wider team, with some nice accessories to put around the office to prove he had done what was needed. She knew in her heart this was not going to work!

'It's all a bit of a flop,' said Colin. 'Too superficial, too rushed, and no one believes it anyway because we still get stuck between the sales and purchasing tug of war!' He raised his hand to whisper conspiratorially behind it: 'People say it's like putting a sticking plaster on a broken arm – useless!'

Colin slithered off and Bobbi was left to her thoughts. 'Poor Phil, his heart is in the right place, but he is not in control of his environment. He needs Gavin's help to resolve that situation. Until he gets that, he'll have conflicting priorities and not enough time. He doesn't have or create the time to have a meaningful relationship with his team, so there is no connection, and everything feels forced, or insincere. It's just liked a new plant with shallow roots, with no substance it easily shrivels and dies.' It *strengthened her resolve to get to a position where she could help resolve some of these issues and make the company less dysfunctional.*

Bobbi's meeting with Sue went as planned. It was structured, amiable, stretching, challenging, with an opportunity to learn and ultimately motivating. She marvelled again as she was leaving the office on a high – what a great return on that 0.5 per cent investment. They had chatted through what Colin had talked about and Sue had challenged her, saying, 'Knowing all the pressures on Phil, how would you have approached it differently to get the message across?' It was a fair challenge, thought Bobbi. It's always easy to judge others without putting yourself in their shoes! 'I think the personal touch is the key to important communication,' she replied. 'No-one could have predicted the operational challenge that broke up the meeting, but he could have delayed briefing it a few days and reconvened the team before or after work to finalise everyone's input. Alternatively, if he felt he had enough feedback and could pull the brief together himself then he should have delivered it personally. Get the wider team in half an hour early, lay on some coffee and cakes from Black & White, and take the time to show them that you care about what you're communicating. People will filter an email through their own lenses of optimism, pessimism or cynicism, and they will do the same with personal communications too, but at least you can see their faces and gauge their reactions. You can also answer immediate questions and, most importantly, transmit your passion and commitment in what you're talking about. That's worth a thousand emails,' said Bobbi animatedly. 'Even if you're the biggest introvert and hate speaking in public, your team will know that and will place all the more trust in what you're saying, as they know what it's costing you to say it. People don't want to be entertained with slick presentations, they just want the truth, delivered with integrity.'

'Quite right,' said Sue. 'I hope you remember these lessons for your teams in the future. No matter how much time you think it takes up, that you can't spare, it's a great investment that will save you ten times the amount of time in the future, and deliver better results in the meantime.'

Bobbi was walking to the Tube, past the hubbub of Black & White. It seemed particularly full and happy tonight. As sometimes happened, she felt guilty as she experienced a pang of jealousy. 'I know it's a small place, not a big office,' she thought, 'and it may be different if I visited the other branches of Black & White (although she suspected it would be the same!) but they always seem a REAL team. Working together, helping one another, communicating happily, focused on the customer and creating a great atmosphere. Was it possible to take that vibe and replicate it in a large widespread corporation?' Bobbi wondered. 'I don't know,' she answered herself, 'but I'm determined that if I get the opportunity then that's what I will aim to do.'

She saw Scott who gave her a wave. 'Not today,' she thought. 'I've got loads of actions and research to do following my development meeting and I just want to get home and get on with it.' She waved back and shook her head apologetically then strode off purposefully toward the Tube station.

Terra Nova Review

Now review that situation and think about it in the context of your own business or team – what can you learn and apply or change?

Specifically:
- What did Sue do that helped Bobbi feel valued?
- What mistakes did Phil make?

- *What can you learn about how to nurture your team?*

- *Think of your key people. Do you think they feel valued and that they are being developed?*

- *What can you do TODAY to improve this situation?*

CHAPTER SUMMARY

To *nurture* means to care for and protect something while it's growing. For you, that's all about your team and your dream, and the way to do it is simply by aligning the way you treat them in the same way as you would treat your children.

Without nurturing your team and your business they won't grow strong and become independent, resulting in failure, either immediately or over time.

Firstly, protect your team and your dreams. Be present, be available, and prioritise time with them. Ensure that the roots of growth and development are strong and that they're regularly 'fed' with good positive information and support.

Ensure that you're training, developing and coaching your team. Just as you may teach your son to play football from a very basic level, through until his skills are better than yours, and then you might get specialist coaching – pass on all your knowledge to your team, help, and encourage them to develop, and then look to invest in specialist training where appropriate to further hone and develop their skills. This training is not a cost, it's an investment, and will pay you back handsomely over time.

Next, ensure that you embed your culture, values and belief in the team and the business. Just as you would ensure that your family understood your core beliefs and principles, keep living the values and reinforcing them within your team.

Finally, 'if you love them, set them free'. Develop your team and their skills to the level that they become independent and can work and develop in line with the company goals without your constant guidance and supervision. We long to prepare our children to be self-sufficient and stand on their own two feet, so do the same with your team and your business so that you can focus on new growth and opportunities.

A key difference between team and family is that you can change your team. A point to note is that if despite all your nurturing, training, guidance and investment, a team member is not developing, growing or even supporting the vision, then you should look to change that team member and bring in someone who has talents to share and who is committed to the dreams for the business. I always see this as a last resort. I prefer to promote from within, from a pool of people who have lived the vision and values, but sometimes you may need to strengthen the team or recruit for a specific skill that's missing. Ensure that this is done with the vision and values in mind and that the person will complement and strengthen the team.

NEXT STEPS

I want you to have a look at your team and assess its capabilities. You need to identify if, as a team, you're missing any key skills. Notice how much assistance and development each member needs.

Construct a grid for each person as below. The list is an example. You can expand or reduce it as you wish. Against each measure, assess whether the individual delivers on a scale of 1-4. Use the following as a guide: 1: Not at all; 2: Partially; 3: Acceptable delivery; and, 4: Outstanding delivery.

Check all the core skills that you think you need in the team, and on the table highlight their core skill and whether they deliver against it. You may find that across your team you don't cover all the core skills you need, in which case you need to recruit to your team. Or you may find that a skill is covered by two team members and you need to decide how to manage that – either it is divisible into sub-skills which they share, or you need to have it as a key development for one of the team to broaden their abilities to cover the skill on their own.

If you're happy that you have all the core skills required, you can review where each of your team is on the matrix, and that will form the basis of the discussions you can have with them to help develop, support, nurture, and train them.

Do they deliver	1	2	3	4
Vision				
Values				
Core Skills				
Teamwork				
Desire				
Potential				
Risk				

Let's take Dave as an example. He looks after social media in the business. His review may look like this:

Do they deliver	1	2	3	4
Vision			X	
Values		X		
Core Skills (social media)				X
Teamwork	X			
Desire			X	
Potential			X	
Risk		X		

We can look at how we may want to nurture Dave in his career.

- He supports the vision of the business but doesn't always demonstrate the values.

- He is excellent at his job on social media.

- He is a bit of a loner and not a great team player.

- He has a desire to get on and he has good potential.

- It wouldn't be a huge risk if he left.

So, looking at that on the positive side we can talk to Dave about how pleased we are that he supports the vision of the business and what a fantastic job he does. We could discuss whether he requires or desires any additional specialist training, how that might work, likely cost, benefit to the business and Dave, and so on. We can discuss his desire to progress and how we can help him realise his potential. On the development side, we need to give examples of where he hasn't demonstrated the values of the business and why it's important to do so, and whether he may require some refresher training. Also, we can discuss the benefits and importance of teamwork and how he may play a bigger part within the team.

We should diarise regular meetings with Dave to discuss these views. We should get his feedback, agree on actions we're both going to take, and then review progress against these actions. We must endeavour to stick to the meetings to show Dave how valued he is and how important his development is to us and the business.

Doing this review for all your team, sticking to the timings and delivering on the actions will transform the speed and quality of the development of your team. You can finally let them be free to deliver against the goals of the business whilst you move on to create new growth and revenue opportunities.

CHAPTER 4

Increase everything

* * * * *

'Average assumes—incorrectly, of course—that everything operates stably. People optimistically overestimate how well things will go and then underestimate how much energy and effort it will take just to push things through. Anyone who has made it in business will support this concept.'
- Grant Cardone (American billionaire entrepreneur)

* * * * *

What is it?

In his book *The 10X Rule,* Grant Cardone states that there are four responses to every situation or challenge

1. Retreat

2. Do nothing

3. Take a normal level of action usually required

4. Take MASSIVE levels of action

The basic assertion is that people generally underestimate the amount of action that's needed to achieve the goals they set – whether that be the size of the action, the strength of the action, or the persistence of the action, we generally underestimate what we need.

As a result, we sit there six months later and wonder why we're not where we wanted or expected to be.

* * * * *

'No battle plan survives the first encounter with the enemy'. (Anon)

* * * * *

It's a fact that things will go wrong, unexpected things will happen, some things may go significantly better and quicker than expected, but in any event, we will need to tweak our plans.

The principle of 'increasing everything' is following that general principle of 10X laid out by Grant Cardone, that we will need to go further, try harder, pursue longer, and move quicker than we originally anticipated.

You have three choices –

1. Launch the plan or strategy and be prepared to increase everything to a greater level to achieve success.

2. Plan accordingly that you will need to do more than expected, and proactively build that into your original execution (this is just an enhanced version of the first choice!).

3. Launch the plan, and regardless of how successful or unsuccessful

it is, and regardless of how many incorrect assumptions you've made, and regardless of changing economic or market circumstances – just stick rigidly to the plan. (Even reading that sentence must enable you to see what a bad choice that one is!)

Why is it important?

Quite simply, if you don't try to increase everything, you will, by default, reduce everything! Business is not an experiment that's performed under laboratory conditions – it's a living, breathing organism that exists in the real world. Customers react to what you offer, competitors react to what you're doing, the regulatory and economic conditions that you operate within are constantly changing. If you don't move, you go backwards, you get overtaken. If you don't increase, others increase around you and you end up being less relevant, smaller and less competitive.

A great business skill is recognising and capitalising upon momentum! If you have momentum, then keep it, and grow it. If you don't have momentum, then try to create it. If you have an advantage, double down on it. If your competitors have an advantage, then do what you can to overhaul it. Don't stand still. Don't shrink and die.

There's a real temptation if things are working to leave them alone, or if they aren't working, to give them time to work. Try to resist those temptations and increase everything. It will make an unbelievable difference to your business and your growth and success – don't hold back.

How do I do it?

'So, "increase everything" sounds like great advice,' you say. 'Can you be a little more specific?'

In general, the key areas that are usually underestimated in any plan are the ones laid out below. If you can build these areas into your plan for extra attention, then you stand a greater chance of success.

People are often concerned that by doing this, their plan becomes too cautious or too expensive, but generally speaking, it just becomes more realistic!

You will know yourself best, but most of us, especially on projects or plans that we're passionate about, are too optimistic and too 'rose-tinted' in our views, critiques and expectations.

So, my recommendation is, in all these areas, cast a critical eye over your plans, bounce them off a partner or mentor for alternative opinions or ask someone you trust to help you 'stress test' some adverse scenarios.

1. Time

It may sound obvious, but generally, we assume that progress, action, or success will happen quicker than it actually does. This may be as a result of several of the points referred to later, or just due to naïve optimism on our part. Whatever the reason, time generally costs money, and you need to plan for the organisation to run for a longer time than planned on poorer financial performances. Can the business stand it? What is the impact on cash flow? Do you need some cash contingencies?

Time is a fairly simple one to assess as you can model the impact of improvements taking two or three times longer to come to fruition and ensure that the business is robust enough to withstand that, or plan to have a contingency in place.

2. Capital/Working capital

The second area generally underestimated is the amount of capital investment or working capital investment needed to achieve the success anticipated.

The amount of working capital (cash, stock, creditors, debtors) needed may be an outworking of the first point – it just takes longer. Alternatively, you could be too optimistic on payment terms, or stock turn for new products, etc.

Capital investment in fixed assets should be relatively easy to forecast correctly, but people often underestimate the return on investment either in scale or speed.

In both of these areas, it should be relatively straightforward to model some alternative scenarios and ensure that the finances are strong enough to cope with some variance or have a contingency plan in place.

3. Human resources

Don't assume that everyone is going to be as hardworking, productive and passionate as you or your existing team. Don't underestimate the amount of inbuilt knowledge that exists, that new employees will have to learn.

If you're planning a project that engages new employees, then assume lower productivity, longer training periods, and higher staff turnover than currently exists. This will impact costs and efficiencies so ensure that you look at how would you cope with variances in both these areas.

Within human resources also live human relationships. If you expand a team and start to share a vision, it may take a longer time than you expect to coach and guide your team to be as passionate and committed to the vision as you are. You will need to invest more of your energy and commitment to ensure that the urgency and clarity are shared amongst the team.

Unless you're incredibly fortunate, you probably won't have a 100 per cent success rate on recruitment and retention as well, and you need to factor in the time effect of staff turnover, recruitment and training into your plans.

4. Stakeholders and influencers

There will be more people or organisations that have an interest in or can have an influence on your project or vision than you think.

Think through your plan or your goal. Consider all the people influenced positively or negatively by it. Consider what their reactions may be if you're successful. What will the impact on your competitors be, how will they react and who can they galvanise in support?

Will your project have implications for employees? Do you need to consider trade union reactions or industry bodies?

Do you need to influence governmental thinking or any not-for-profit organisations?

Think as broadly as possible of all potential stakeholders and influencers and ensure that you consider them in your plans.

5. Communications

I guarantee that you will need to increase your communication plans.

Internal communications are vital to ensure that the vision is clear, the team are aligned, the objectives are known, etc. It's amazing how much you need to communicate. It's amazing how two people hearing the same message can reach completely different interpretations – but they do.

You need to plan to communicate frequently, consistently and through a variety of mediums.

This will be covered in detail in the next chapter.

External communications are just as vital. The biggest threat to many businesses is anonymity. The world is huge and the multimedia messages are constant, varied, and relentless.

You may feel that you're over-communicating and that people may become sick of you. I can almost guarantee that this will never happen – but that the opposite is far more likely. If you don't communicate, they will have no idea who you are, what you stand for, and what you're trying to achieve.

Again, we will cover the detail of this in the next chapter.

Never Say, 'If only!' Only Ask, 'What if?'

Everything that happens to your product, project or service is your responsibility. Anything your competitors and customers do is your responsibility. Every way that your employees and stakeholders act is your responsibility. That's a bit harsh, isn't it? How can you be responsible for all the actions of these disparate groups – you don't know what they're going to do, it's outside of your control. Well – yes and no!

I don't want to hear people in my business saying, 'if only!'

- If only our competitor hadn't done that.
- If only our employees hadn't reacted that way.
- If only the customers had stayed longer.
- If only this promotion had worked.
- If only the economy hadn't slowed down 5 per cent last year.
- If only, if only, if only!

The only reason people say, 'If only' is because they haven't spent enough time asking, 'What if?' As part of your scenario planning and thoughts about mitigating and increasing actions, you should be constantly asking, 'What if?'

- What if our competitor drops their price?
- What if our employees disagree?
- What if our customers leave?
- What if the promotion doesn't work?

- What if demand drops 5 per cent, can we survive?
- What if, what if, what if?

What if? are the two most powerful words you can ask, and they will revolutionise your planning and contingency planning. They will transform your business and allow you to be prepared to increase everything, in the right areas at the right time, based on market circumstances that you have, to a certain extent, thought through.

So, having now planned and stress-tested all these areas and thought about what happens if you need to increase the time, capital, or resources needed, etc., you should be better prepared to launch the project. What you now need to do is review the project weekly and monthly and review all those areas. What has happened? Has it gone as you expected? What has the customer reaction been? What has the competitor reaction been? What have your employees done? Is the communication clear?

Every week and month, go through the whole process again – do I need to increase in this area, is it hitting my expectations, is there more I could do? Increasing everything is a constant vigil, and needs constant review to ensure you stay ahead of the competition and delight your customers and employees.

Riding the Wave of Success

Now, all these areas that I've covered are focused on the need to increase your level of activity in key areas due to lack of traction, and slower than expected progress. But life is not always harder than expected. In many cases, you may have far greater success than you imagined or planned for. Quick adaption of your ideas, better than expected financial results, more new customers, higher sales? Whatever the area of success, my recommendation is again, 'increase everything'. If you have found a sweet spot, exploit it. Don't be too distracted by areas that are behind the plan. By all means, invest in these areas to get them back on track, but not at the expense of your successes. Strengthen your weaknesses but exploit your strengths. Ride the wave of success and see where it takes you – it could help change and refine your plans in the same way (or better way) than a big problem could.

People Often Focus on the Problems to the Exclusion of the Successes

This is a grave error. If something is working, double your efforts in that area, and watch your success multiply.

Elon Musk and Tesla Motors: Increasing Everything Against the Odds

Elon Musk and Tesla would make good and bad examples of many of the aspects being discussed in this book. I did wonder whether to use them for any examples as who knows in ten years time whether they will be one of the world's largest companies or a footnote in history and the subject of endless Harvard case studies. Whatever the answer is, you would be well served by looking at what happened to them.

This example is not an exhaustive study of the pros and cons of Tesla, but an example of how to 'increase everything' Elon Musk style!

Tesla was founded in 2003 with the goal of commercialising electric vehicles. Tesla reported net losses most quarters for many years, but surprised investors in Q3 2019 with a $143m net profit.

The company started with a typical technology strategy rather than an automobile strategy. They targeted affluent early adopters with the early models and then used the revenue from them to reinvest into more mainstream models as they progressed. They started with the Roadster, invested that revenue into the Model S, then onto the Model X, then the more affordable Model 3 and Model Y. According to Musk, new technology in any field takes a few versions to optimise before reaching the mass market, and in the case of Tesla, it's competing with 150 years and trillions of dollars spent on developing internal combustion engine cars.

If one looks at the production numbers for Tesla, it shows a steady start and recent acceleration.

Quarter	Year	Cars Produced
1	2013	5,000
1	2014	6,500
1	2015	10,000
1	2016	15,000
1	2017	25,000
1	2018	30,000
1	2019	63,000
1	2020	103,000

The amazing thing is that Musk was able to keep Tesla doing this whilst never making a penny. He sold the inspirational vision to shareholders and banks and investors who kept the faith, and time will tell if that faith is rewarded.

Year	Revenue	Profit
2015	$4.05 Bn	($0.89 Bn)
2016	$7.01 Bn	($0.67 Bn)
2017	$11.76 Bn	($1.96 Bn)
2018	$21.46 Bn	($0.98 Bn)
2019	$24.30 Bn	($0.75 Bn)

Despite the losses, Musk communicated the inspirational vision and kept the investors onside while he kept increasing everything that he saw as important: design expenditure, research into developing better battery technology, and resource and expenditure on innovation. He kept making losses but kept increasing sales targets, outlets, and dealers. Even when he was losing money on every car sold, he kept increasing sales. He knew he needed the sales to create the volume to expand into more mainstream cars, which is when he saw profitability coming with the Model 3 and Model Y.

He continually increased investment in production. They started in Fremont with cars, then Reno and Buffalo with battery production. Then he built a factory in Shanghai for both cars and battery production, and most recently Berlin for battery production and maybe cars in the future.

He raised $19 billion of funding and had $9 billion of negative cash flow, but still, he kept increasing everything. Short sellers were hovering over the stock price, waiting to take the company down, but still, he increased everything.

Will he be proved right or wrong? I don't know, but no-one can ever accuse Elon Musk of playing it safe. He definitely increases everything (not to mention creating hyperloop transportation systems and attempting to travel to space!). If Elon reads the copy of my book, I will send him then hopefully he will realise that over time you need to continue to back the winning strategies, embed them into your business and cull the losing ideas – that's the pathway to accelerated and continued success!

Terra Nova Business Solutions

Bobbi was on edge. She hadn't slept well and was nervously walking down to the office. It was one of those rare days when she decided to pop into Black & White on the way into work rather than only afterwards. It wasn't too busy, and she chatted to Gill as she made her latte.

'You're looking a little stressed if you don't mind my saying,' Gill enquired, with genuine concern. 'Yes, a little,' Bobbi replied, playing down her real feelings. 'It's a big day at work. I've been on this cross-functional project team for ages. We developed a new initiative for a fresh income stream for the business, and the initiative has been running for six months now. Today is the day we present the six-month progress report to the sponsors and the CEO. It's been hard work but a great experience. I suppose I'm stressed because it's been a little frustrating with a lack of clear guidance and conflicting priorities. I'm hoping that today is the day when we can show how things are going and get some definitive guidance on the way forward.'

'Wow, sounds like a big day – this one is on the house, you need it! Are the others sharing your pain?' Gill asked.

'I seem to be more frustrated than the others,' Bobbi replied. 'The longer serving employees just accept it as the way things are, which is quite sad. I hope I never end up like that! Thanks for the pick-me-up!' Bobbi smiled as she left with her coffee to get to the office to prepare. She reached her desk and started to review the presentation and notes that the team were going to run through with Penny, Terry and Gavin.

The team had come up with a diversification plan, taking Terra Nova's core B2B (business to business) competencies and attempting to translate them into a B2C (business to consumer) offering. Given the growth in the relatively well-off elderly section of society, they thought that their core offerings like cleaning, maintenance, landscaping, security and so on would be attractive to private individuals, as well as less obvious offerings like chauffeuring, and personal assistant (PA) services. It was obviously a reasonably competitive market, but they felt that with the Terra Nova brand strength behind the offering it should be reassuring and attractive to the target market. They also offered an easy-to-use online portal to access all the services, see your booking, check the status, and so on. They had branded the business as TerraNova2U.co.uk and they felt that it was going pretty well overall. It was better in the areas on landscaping and surprisingly to Bobbi, PA services, but not doing so well in cleaning and chauffeuring. Cleaning was a surprise as they expected that to be the main part of the business.

The meeting time came. It was one of the few times Bobbi had been in the boardroom in her first year at the business. It seemed pretty slick she thought – polished chrome, smoked glass, a big industrial effect board table and comfy sleek leather chairs. 'I could definitely work in this environment,' she thought.

The atmosphere in the room, however, was decidedly NOT cool. It felt edgy, the group were nervous, and this only increased when Terry and Penny entered with their traditional appearance of looking like they had just finished an argument and were both still fretting over it. Gavin breezed in after them, seemingly oblivious to any undercurrent, and was a torrent of charm – welcoming everyone in the room individually, knowing all their names, shaking their hand, and having a bit of small talk with each of them. Amazingly, he lifted the mood of the whole room. 'He's smooth, I will give him that,' thought Bobbi admiringly.

The team presented. Bobbi thought it went well and everyone played their part perfectly. They waited for some feedback.

Terry was the first in as usual. 'Well, it seems ok, well done, but chauffeuring and cleaning seem to be a waste of time with no real demand. Let's stop those services now, save some money, and see if we can get this thing into profit as soon as possible.'

Penny sighed and rolled her eyes. When she spoke, her voice carried an air of exasperation. 'Cleaning is our core business, it's our roots, and loads of people use cleaners. We must be able to make that area work, and chauffeuring seems like a logical service offering in today's more mobile and flexible society. I say we keep them going. But as ever you're focused on the negatives. Look at landscaping, which is flying, and PA services are doing way more than we expected them to. We should capitalise on this and invest more to secure our position.'

'Spend, spend, spend,' retorted Terry. 'I'm glad we don't share a bank account! Look, I don't mind putting some of the savings from cutting the nonperforming areas into growing the successful ones faster, but not putting

in extra money — we still haven't seen a penny of profit from this venture you know.'

'What new venture sees a profit in six months?' groaned Penny. 'This is about planning for the next five years, not five minutes!'

The to and fro of the argument continued while Gavin seemed almost tuned out as if he wasn't listening. Eventually, he leaned forward and Terry and Penny stopped arguing. 'Okay everyone, great job, great work and super progress. Well done. I've listened to both sides of the argument closely and I think the best thing to do at the moment is just to continue as we are, no new money (looking at Penny) but no cutting either (looking at Terry). I'm sure cleaning will come around and we can see if the demand for the other services is sustainable as well. So, let's stick with it for another six months and then review again. Well done once again, team — super job!'

Gavin, Terry and Penny left. Gavin's response when he said it like that seemed perfectly reasonable but afterwards, Bobbi just felt deflated. She decided it was a bit of a 'Goldilocks' response — not too hot, not too cold, just boringly conservatively, averagely stuck in the middle! In fact, on reflection that seemed to be his approach to most tough decisions. She was starting to sadly realise that he had loads of charm and charisma but was severely lacking in steel and substance. 'But on the positive side,' she thought, 'it's another six months to make a name for myself and get that promotion.'

Bobbi debriefed with the rest of the team and sadly, and unsurprisingly, they all thought it was 'as expected'! Bobbi had hoped that TerraNova2U (TN2U) would breathe new life into the business, but it was in danger of being sucked into the old ways of doing things itself (or not doing things if Gavin had his way), and she was determined not to let that happen.

With the rest of the team, they agreed on responsibilities and actions to proceed and set a review in the next three weeks. 'Today,' thought Bobbi, 'is definitely a Black & White day!'

Julie was away so Bobbi went down on her own. She had left work half an hour early and found the place quite quiet. She had never really been there when it wasn't packed, but it still had a friendly, happy buzz about the place.

One major benefit was that her favourite chair was available, the tattered brown, leather, easy chair just in the corner near the indoor palm tree. She got her drink and sat down with an audible sigh of relief. 'Wow, tough day?' asked Scott who she hadn't noticed was cleaning the table behind her. Bobbi laughed. 'You could say that. Listen, do you have five minutes for a chat? I wanted to ask you how the Old School Roastery project was going.' Scott looked around to check no-one needed anything. 'Sure,' he said. 'Let's beat the rush.'

'So, it's going really well,' enthused Scott. 'Actually, well but mixed would be more realistic. The retail side is flying, we've sold it into loads of delis and local shops, into offices (like yours), and even into some coffee shops in other areas. We are actually struggling to keep up with the demand. Obviously, on the back of that, donations to local school projects are up as well, which is great. Where we're struggling a little is in the area of engagement with excluded kids and getting them into vocational training. We've had a few successes but no matter how 'cool' we think we may be; we're struggling to connect with them when we try to explain the concept. Once they agree to participate, it's great but getting them interested is the struggle.'

'Interesting,' thought Bobbi. 'Its patchy success is a bit like TN2U.'

'So, what are you planning to do?' she asked, genuinely interested.

'Well, we discussed it at the managers' coffee club last week,' replied Scott. 'We decided the first thing to do is double down on our successes. We'll employ two extra full-time people at the roastery to increase production. They will be two of our vocational training graduates and, specifically, two of the harder ones we've had. This will mean more of an investment in time to manage them, but it will be worth it for the benefit they'll bring the wider scheme. That increase in employees enables increased production, increased sales, and increased money to schools, so that'll be great. Secondly, what we'll do is use the two new employees to work three days a week in the roastery, and two days a week as influencers, reaching out to excluded kids and showing them the reality of what is possible. We think this will work really well as the initiative will be so much more compelling from someone who has been through it. That's also why we chose two real hard cases, as their original situation will be worse than most of those they're reaching out to. The roastery team have agreed that they can cover the kids being out for two days a week and still just reach the original plans in terms of production, and indeed the graduates are so pleased that they're saying they will come back in after a day of meeting with other kids to do some work in the roastery as well. Hopefully, that will work and it's a great way to see the team pulling together.'

Bobbi, as was often the case, was amazed at how the small coffee shop chain got management decisions so right whilst her publicly quoted company failed!

She spoke thoughtfully, 'So, you're increasing investment where you're successful, building on your strengths, and using that extra strength to also improve the areas where you're performing less well. An improvement in one area leads to an improvement in the other area, and you get two successes instead of one! That's real positive synergy.'

'I hadn't thought of it quite like that,' said Scott, 'but positive synergy is a great brand name for our new coffee blend we're planning to launch – a single estate arabica from Tanzania where one-third of the profits go back to building schools in the local community. We were looking for a good name – I think Positive Synergy might be it, I love it. I will suggest it to the owner.'

Bobbi laughed (secretly pleased that she had stumbled across a good brand idea). Scott saw that a few more people had come in and made his apologies. 'Sorry, I need to get serving, great to chat!' 'Yes, it was,' said Bobbi. 'Let's do it again sometime.' They exchanged an awkward glance, and Scott rushed off to help some customers.

Bobbi finished her drink whilst contemplating the decisive benefit of building on one's strengths to also help areas of weakness, versus the indecisive 'status quo' they had reached in her own meeting today. She sighed silently and picked up a leaflet on the Old School Roastery project to read more about the updates.

Terra Nova Review

Now review that situation and think about it in the context of your own business or team – what can you learn and apply or change?

Specifically:

- *What were the options with TN2U, and which would you have chosen?*

- *Do you think they will learn anything with the plan they have taken?*

- *What do you think of the Old School Roastery approach?*

- *Can you see any similarities in the decisions you face or have faced?*

- *Pick an area or two where you can take instant action. What can you do TODAY to make a difference in your approach?*

CHAPTER SUMMARY

Increase everything or see everything decrease! Grant Cardone highlights the following four typical reactions to every situation:

- Retreat

- Do nothing

- Take normal amounts of action

- Take MASSIVE action

If you don't try to increase everything then you will end up going backwards as the marketplace and your competition overtake you.

As it is written, 'No plan survives the first contact with the enemy', or as the former boxer Mike Tyson less eloquently put it, 'Everyone has a plan until they get punched in the face'!

When you start an initiative or product or service, you should be looking at all areas and thinking through different scenarios and anticipating 'what if' scenarios so that you can help to futureproof your plans.

The more time you spend thinking 'what if?', the less time you will spend saying 'if only!'

The key areas you need to focus on increasing and stress testing are

- Time – allocation of it and time given to succeed
- Capital – investment capital and working capital
- Human resources – enough people, the right people, correctly motivated and directed people
- Stakeholders and influencers – is everyone engaged and on board? Do I need to do more?
- Communications – you can NEVER over-communicate

NEXT STEPS

Like many of the plans in 'Next Steps', the solution is found in a table. I find it incredibly helpful to get a range of diverse ideas, topics and data into one place. You can get a better overall view and also have some discipline and structure in your planning and ensure you aren't missing anything.

Increase Everything applies to a communications plan, a sales strategy, a project, a product launch, or anything you want to look at. In each instance, you will need to adapt the plan here, but the principles will be the same.

Imagine that I own a confectionery business and we have launched a new protein chocolate bar called 'JACKED!'

A three-month review shows a mixed performance on the KPI's we want to look at. By creating the 'Performance and Action Table', we can quickly see where we're doing well and have some momentum, and also where we have some disparity to our original forecast. The table ensures that we allocate actions to areas of success and not just focus on our problems. It also highlights areas where we have conflicting information that will need further investigation.

Item	3 Month Budget	3 Month Actual	Action Plan
Sales	£1,000,000	£800,000	Dissect sales by channel and see if it is sector specific or overall Review the quality of the sales team by channel – is there a correlation? Change the sales team structure if necessary Review and improve sales commission scheme if necessary
Margin	25%	23%	Production costs are lower but margins are lower so we must be struggling to achieve targeted selling prices – investigate reasons, aligned with sales capabilities. Increase coverage in all channels with more experienced accompaniment to ensure we hit target pricing

Production Cost	10%	9%	Don't accept this as good enough Could it be 8 per cent, where are the key variances? Was there a cheap deal on utilities or raw materials that are masking the true figure? Increase investigation into production efficiencies but remember to celebrate success with the team
Raw Material Cost	5%	3%	Don't accept this as good enough Any major commodity price fluctuations that could also go the other way? Are the ingredients too cheap and affecting the customers' quality perception maybe giving the low sales? Increase consumer research to understand. Celebrate success with the team and increase efforts on recipe engineering to lower costs further without compromising taste
Advertising Budget	£250,000	£250,000	Okay, but could it have been bought more effectively? Review the media and target audiences to ensure we're targeting the correct segments of the population

Advertising Effectiveness Rating	8	7	Clearly needs improvement. As above, were we not targeting the correct publications for the target market, or was the execution of the advertising not effective? Increase efforts to understand what is driving this
Social Media Followers	20,000	30,000	A good performance. Instagram especially appears to be working well and engaging with the target market Double resource allocation on Instagram and drive this success even harder. Maybe a better long-term option than advertising Increase understanding of how to translate this Instagram success to other social media platforms

As I said, you can adapt the Performance and Action Table to your specific needs but I strongly recommend you adopt this approach. It will help you to capture actions in all areas and will also help you to see where conflicting or overlapping areas may need more investigation (e.g. lower margin versus lower production costs, etc).

CHAPTER 5

Tell, Tell, Tell

* * * * *

'The biggest single problem in communication is the illusion that it has taken place.' – George Bernard Shaw (Playwright)

* * * * *

A 2014 Gallop Survey in the United States reported the very disturbing fact that 46 per cent of employees rarely, or never, leave a meeting knowing what they're supposed to do next.

Other interesting communication facts include the following:

- Only one out of three emails are opened.

- 49 per cent of millennials support social tools for workplace collaboration.

- Productivity improves by up to 25 per cent in organisations with connected employees (that's to say, an employee who is emotionally involved and engaged with the aims of the business).

- Twenty-eight per cent of people reported poor communication as the primary cause for failing to deliver a project within the original timeframe.

- Ninety-seven per cent of employees believe communication has an impact on tasks performed every day.

(Source - Bluesource UK 2018)

This demonstrates that knowing how to communicate in the right way, at the right time, and engaging your team with inspiring and relevant information is critical to delivering world-class performance, and indeed, the absence of it will result in substandard performance from a disengaged team.

What is it?

We've surely all been in situations, companies, or even families where we have experienced poor communication. I'm sure we could all quote a tragic or amusing story. The various findings at the start of this chapter show that good communication is probably THE most important contribution to creating and delivering success. An average plan communicated to an engaged workforce in an excellent and energising way will always be far more successful than the most amazing, innovative, and insightful plan communicated badly.

In my experience, communication is the one thing that you cannot overdo.

As I will explain, the act of talking or writing does not mean you're communicating. As reflected in the quote at the beginning, the biggest failure is when people assume communication has taken place when it hasn't really. To communicate effectively you need to get the message that you wish to be communicated across to the team that you wish to hear it, in the manner that they need it to be done. After that, you need to check their understanding and collate their feedback. Then you refine and communicate again and again until everything is as you had intended at the beginning.

The reason your crystal-clear goal and message has such a hard time being received, understood, and adopted by your team is due to the number of factors that can negatively impact the message. When you consider the number of individual factors that can have an effect and the mathematical combination of all these multiple factors, then the number of permutations of interpretation are almost infinite. I will explain this further but for example, each of the following will have a different impact on each person you are communicating with: their mood, the environment, the time of day, their personal distractions away from work, their world view, your mood, your assumptions, your method of communicating and so on. No wonder so many attempts at communication fail.

Why is it important?

There are six key ways in which good communication contributes to the success of your business or venture:

1. Speed

The clearer your communication, the more consistent it is, and the more often you repeat it, the quicker your team and the wider team will understand and act upon the message. We all know that people need to hear a message more than once, generally speaking, to remember it. 'Effective Frequency' is a term used to describe the number of times a person needs to hear an advertising message in order to respond to it. There are different views from different experts as to what that number is, but the most famous one is probably the 'Rule of 7' which states that consumers need to hear your message seven times before they consider taking action.

Now, communicating within your business is not quite the same as advertising because hopefully the team are already engaged and bought into the process, but I see no reason why you would not aim for many repetitions, maybe as many as seven, of your key messages just in case people aren't bought in or haven't heard anything before because they're new starters and so on.

The more your team have a common understanding, and the quicker you're able to do that, then the quicker you will see results and success.

2. Consistency

As far as possible, using just one message prevents misinterpretation and accidental or deliberate manipulation of the key things you're trying to communicate. I'm sure many of you have played 'Chinese whispers' or 'broken telephone' at a children's party (if not then look it up). It shows that communication, when passed from person to person, changes the key message based on what people hear, or think they hear, or don't really hear, in which case they'll make it up.

The apocryphal tale of the army battalion in WWI tells that they needed reinforcements as they were going to attack the enemy. The message went back through several runners passing the message from man to man. The message started as 'Send reinforcements, we're going to advance' but by the time it reached the general back at headquarters he was told, 'Send three and fourpence, we're going to a dance'! Needless to say, no support was sent.

Making sure everyone has one version of the truth is vital to the smooth running of any business or project and is all down to good communication. This is especially important when you have decentralised teams, particularly if they're in different countries with different first languages. Always ensure your message means what you want it to mean when it has been translated. An amusing (if you weren't involved) story regarding Pepsi proves the point. In the 1960s, Pepsi was looking to break into the Chinese market and translated its slogan into Mandarin. The slogan at the time was 'Come Alive with Pepsi', however, the translated slogan came out as 'Pepsi brings your ancestors back from the grave'! Unsurprisingly, this lost them a lot of business in the region.

3. Reinforcing the message

This is essentially a mixture of points one and two. When you learn a new language on CD or an app, they continually bring you back to words or phrases you have learned before. Initially every lesson, then every few lessons, then every ten lessons. This phased and delayed repetition keeps your memory sharp with eventually only a rare reminder. That's the way to keep your message consistent and alive.

4. Motivating the team

This especially applies in the case of the geographically diverse teams. If you aren't there all the time to recognise and celebrate success, reinforce the key messages and update the team on progress, then it becomes easy for people to feel disenfranchised and left out of the team. Communication is key to keep people engaged, and not just messaging, but also interacting through polls, surveys, questionnaires and the like. A motivated team, with the same understanding and goals, will obviously outperform one that isn't. That's blindingly obvious, but you would be amazed by how many times people let the situation drift, purely down to lack of communication.

5. Ensuring compliance

Communication is not one-way. As well as sharing the key messages you can gain structured feedback and ensure people are completing tasks in the right way at the right time. Compliance is a key part of consistency. As well as a consistent message, you can ensure consistent execution of the plan.

6. Gaining intelligence

This chapter should be titled 'Tell, Tell, Tell, Ask, Ask, Ask, Listen, Listen, Listen' (but that's not very catchy).

As I said above, communication is a two-way process and if you're making the effort to do it properly, don't just tell people the key messages but ask for feedback on what they think, whether it's working, what can be improved and how you might do it differently. Importantly, when you get the feedback – LISTEN! People at the frontline know way more than people in head office. Not necessarily in terms of strategy or goals, but in terms of what customers and employees think, how people react to the product or service, and how it can be improved. Very often they aren't asked, or if they're asked, people don't listen to the answers.

Wherever I've worked I've always encouraged an employee 'Bright Idea' scheme, whereby anyone at any level can submit ideas on how to improve the business. Many of them will be simple and transactional ideas but occasionally they will lead to great breakthroughs, and most importantly people feel engaged and listened to. We always respond to people to thank them for their idea, and if it will be acted upon or not (and why not). We may reward them with a voucher or a bottle of wine, or if it's a big idea, we get them involved in working on the project.

If you don't communicate effectively, you will limit your success. I'm not saying that you won't have success, but you will not have it to the magnitude that you could have had. A demonstrable example of how communication grows awareness and success is clear if you take a look at the difference that social media makes. Look at a great old footballer like Pele, and then compare his profile and earnings to someone like Lionel Messi. Clearly, there's a lot more money in football nowadays, but 'Messi' the brand, is huge compared to 'Pele'. Don't start an argument over who's the better player, but instead marvel at the scale, scope, and magnitude of Messi and the image he creates, communicated daily on Twitter, Instagram, and YouTube, etc. The frequency and variety of communication make a massive difference to his endorsements and sponsorship revenues.

Your business has the communication tools of the 21st century, so don't behave as if you operate in the 1970s.

Your business will be slower if you communicate poorly, and your team will waste time doing the wrong thing, or the right thing in the wrong way. This is what happens when you get diverse messages or different versions of the truth, whether done accidentally or on purpose. Imagine a tug of war with a big five-stranded rope. If the rope is entwined and everyone is pulling together you can see how much more powerful that is versus the rope being untwisted and five people pulling each strand off in different directions. That's the power of good teamwork and communication versus bad communication and teamwork.

Your team will be demotivated if you communicate poorly. People are regularly asking themselves (usually on a Monday morning!) 'Why am I doing this?', 'What's the point?', 'What am I meant to be doing?', 'Am I doing this right?', 'How is the company doing?', and so on. If you aren't answering these questions then clarity will fade, motivation will decline, and people will make their own answer up and lead to the diverse messaging. Think what your team want to know every day, week or month – and make sure you TELL THEM!

Finally, a lack of market intelligence to amend your plans and strategy will, at best, limit the success you will have as you won't fully understand the market dynamics. At worst, it may lead to absolute failure as you don't pick up some critical change that alters the base assumptions upon which you operate. You may have regular research or reviews in place, but as I said above, the frontline intelligence is often quicker, more direct, and more truthful – ignore it at your peril.

How do I do it?

I'm going to consider some of the key factors that can influence the effectiveness of your communication, and also some ideas to help mitigate their impact. Hopefully, they'll give you a checklist to vastly improve your communication – but rest assured, it still won't be perfect!

Unsurprisingly, good communication starts with you! Do you have a clear vision? Is it clear to other people? Can you explain it simply to your partner, your friends, or even your kids? Do you have a thirty-second 'elevator pitch' that you could use to summarise your vision or plan to a stranger during an elevator ride?

Is the vision or plan in simple language – ensure you aren't using complicated words or even worse, industry jargon, or abbreviations. If you use the latter, then you've already severely limited the likely audience who will understand what you're trying to say.

So, now that you've confirmed that you have a clear, concise, and simple vision to communicate, the next step is to ensure that you've got a consistent basis on which to set off your communication journey.

If your vision is to go from point A to point B, you'll have made a lot of dangerous assumptions already.

- Do people have a common understanding of where point A is?
- Does everyone agree that you're at point A?
- Does everyone understand where point B is?
- Will everyone think that point B is a better place to be than point A?

- Does everyone think it's possible to get to point B from a starting position at point A?

So, before you can accurately communicate your vision, you need to do a lot of work bringing people to the same starting point for the journey.

In this instance, you would need to invest time in explaining where the company currently is, and why. Also, explain why point A is not a great place to be, or why point B is so much better.

Once you have that common understanding then you can start to set out the vision of getting to point B, why it's a good place, why it's achievable, and how you'll achieve it.

This creation of a shared common understanding of the key starting point and situation will vastly increase the effectiveness of your overall communication.

Finally, with regards to your planning, ensure that the journey to the end goal is achievable in a series of believable steps. Simply saying that one day we'll put a man on the moon is inspirational but may be too far for some people to comprehend. In this instance, you need the steps of

- Building a rocket

- Launching a rocket

- Making a rocket that can orbit the earth and re-enter the atmosphere

- Sending a chimp into space and back

- Sending men into space and back

- Landing on the moon

Ensure you keep steps of credibility in your communication and plan to ensure maximum buy-in.

So,   clear message √

          simple language √

          common starting point √

          believable steps √

Now HOW to communicate effectively for best results.

This can be summarised very simply

- Right people

- Right time

- Right place

- Right way

Are you communicating to the right people? If you aren't able to, or or aren't planning to speak to everyone at the same time, then what's your plan? By level of seniority, by department, by geography?

Whatever is right in your situation, give thought to how you cascade the communication to achieve the result you want. Once you've communicated to the first group, people will start to talk, so ensure your first group are really the people you want to talk to first!

Secondly, the right time is *really* important in your communication. If it's a complicated message – do it when people are more alert. If it's bad news – consider the best day and time to deliver that news.

If it's a lengthy message to which you want to have questions and answers from the team – then ensure you allow enough time and don't rush it.

If you're trying to be motivational – don't do the briefing in the lunch hour because this encroaches on people's personal time. Also, don't do the brief at the start of the day and expect them to catch up on the day's work through the rest of the day (especially relevant to shift workers or those doing physical work).

If need be, bring people in early (and pay them!). If the message is that important, then show them how serious you are. If you don't pay them, lay on coffee and cake or do it at the end of the day with pizza!

Whatever you do, ensure that you allow sufficient time and that you respect their personal time to maximise the chances of success.

As well as choosing the right time, and allowing enough time, you need to choose the right place to communicate your message. Confidential messages need confidential locations; involved messages will need comfortable locations without distraction. You may choose your location to emphasise your point – like the site of a new factory or head office you're building. In any event, consider the symbolism, or perceived symbolism of *where* you choose to communicate and think whether that will help or hinder your objectives.

Another key aspect of your communication needs to be consistency. If you're able to do all the communication presentations then that's a great advantage (as long as you observe the consistency of the time, place, method, etc., amongst all the groups).

But what if you don't do all the presentations – maybe there are too many people, or they're too geographically spread? If that's the case, then your objective has to be to minimise the opportunity for the variance of the message.

- Present personally to everyone who will be presenting to others.

- Be prescriptive in terms of time, ambience, atmosphere, etc.

- Be thorough in the slides or accompanying materials to minimise the opportunity for 'freestyle interpretation'.

- If you can, maybe record a video for a consistent delivery direct from you, even in your absence.

- Ensure you collect all the questions from all the locations and communicate all the answers back to all areas equally so that there's only one version of the truth, and the depth of the disclosure isn't dependent upon questioning at an individual level.

The aim has to be for everyone to hear the message in the same way as if they were all in the same room at the same time. As discussed, each person will already be filtering the message differently, so you don't want them all hearing a slightly different message.

A final tip, if you can make it work, is to check understanding. Maybe follow up the communication with a survey or feedback form. This will help you understand which messages have landed and which ones have missed. Then, this will enable you to do targeted follow up communications rather than generic and broad follow-ups.

Tell, Tell and Tell Again

You can never over-communicate, no matter what you may think.

Your team, or your wider workforce, aren't living and breathing your vision like you are. They don't worry about it at night or think about it when they're out on a run.

In short, they don't care – until you make them care. They won't care until they fully understand the passion, the vision, the benefits, the 'WIIFM', and they won't fully know that until you've fully communicated.

Case Study: Bidfood's Values and Key Ingredients

When we created our values, we did it by involving the business in articulating what values it stands for. We had over 50 workshops across the business, facilitated by The Global Growth Institute. We involved people from all types of job role, all geographical parts of the country and all levels of seniority. It was a discussion-based workshop, focused on what makes Bidfood special in their eyes. What's the magic ingredient that makes them enjoy working at the company? Would they still work here if it was voluntary, and if so, what makes them want to do that? At the end of that process, we had a very good understanding of what makes the business different from the competition, and what the key values are that unite and inspire the employees. We were able to group the values and distil them down, and even get them to rhyme for ease of memory!

The values are CARE, SHARE, DARE.

Care – Take pride in what you do no matter what you do.

Share – Work together to make great things happen.

Dare – Take brave steps to deliver extraordinary results.

The great thing is that these are business-grown values, not management-imposed values. We told the teams very clearly what we were trying to achieve, we enabled the teams to have the time to participate by clearing their diaries and booking time off shifts, we created a pleasant environment, we facilitated the discussion – and then we LISTENED. Tell, tell, tell and listen, listen, listen!

These values have had fantastic acceptance by the business – because they were created BY the business.

As well as our values, we created a list of 'key ingredients' (as a food business) that we aim to deliver to our customers

- Great food

- Real value

- Service excellence

- Best team

- Forward-thinking

These are key things that we know our customers look for and that we believe we deliver better than anyone else.

In terms of consistency and repetition in communication, we reference a value or key ingredient in almost every piece of communication we do, both internally and externally. This acts as a subtle flag to the recipients to understand what the communication is referencing and how it fits in, and it also reinforces the values and key ingredients constantly. See the example earlier in my internal letter, and we constantly reference it in social media posts, ending with #bestteam, #forwardthinking, #greatfood, etc.

Telling clearly, listening carefully, and communicating constantly is vital to get your messages across in all that you do.

Terra Nova Business Solutions

Bobbi looked at her reflection in the mirror in the lady's restrooms. She had been in the office since 05h30 and it was still quiet now at 07h15. 'I look tired,' she thought. 'Too much work, too little sleep and definitely not enough fun!'

Work had certainly taken priority over the last six months. Since the decision (or lack of decision as she saw it) to keep things in TN2U running as before, rather than cutting, and/or investing, Bobbi had taken responsibility for the cleaning element of the TN2U business, trying to ensure that they replicated their business services success in the consumer services sector. It had been a tough six months – travelling the country, speaking to consumers, holding focus groups, understanding the key drivers and the commercial model, and then working with operations to deliver what was needed. It had taken it out of her, she now realised.

Cleaning services may not be 'sexy' but it IS an area that most people need or would want if they could afford it – and there was good money to be made. She was pleased with how the six months had gone. Cleaning was now the leading revenue generator for TN2U, and also returned a profit. She knew that because of it she was definitely seen internally as a rising star within the business and she felt a great sense of self-achievement as she looked at the tired face in the mirror.

What else was it she could see in her eyes? Disillusionment? Acceptance of average? Had she lost some of her spark and zeal? She rubbed her face, willing it away. 'No,' she thought, 'I'm still me. I will strive to change this business. I will not be dragged down to the level of petty squabbles and office gossip epitomised by so many others.'

Bobbi cheered up when she realised Black & White would be open by now. She could go and get her early morning pick-me-up, which recently had changed from a triple shot latte to a kale and ginger smoothie. Today, however, she felt the latte was calling her name! She enjoyed her morning chats with Gill, who she now considered a friend. She had also enjoyed a few dates with Scott, who she now considered a very good friend, she thought, a blush colouring her cheeks.

The Black & White chain had recently opened its fiftieth outlet, and nothing had changed her opinion that it seemed to operate a far better business than Terra Nova, with strong, clear, inspirational leadership (from the mysterious owner she still hadn't met) and engaged and enthused team members. Bobbi got her smoothie to go, and after a brief chat with Gill, returned to her desk. She had quite a few issues to deal with.

In the last six months, the project team had delivered on TN2U. It was now officially a separate business within Terra Nova. Thankfully, in Bobbi's opinion, it reported into Penny, not Terry, and they were currently considering who would be the right person to lead the separate division.

Bobbi was hopeful that her success in delivering change in the cleaning element would stand her in good stead for this opportunity.

They had decided to focus on landscaping, PA services and cleaning as the three core offerings. She was up against John and Lucy respectively who ran those other two areas, for the top job. Unfortunately, chauffeuring hadn't really worked as the demand was variable and it constantly tied up capital in car fleet and needed people on standby, even when they weren't productive. The team had decided to drop that from the offering of TN2U going forwards.

Three weeks ago, there had been a big briefing session to all the staff in Terra Nova. The aim was to officially launch TN2U to the rest of the business and to excite and engage everyone with the new opportunity. The foundations of the briefing were solid. The team had agreed on the key messages with Penny and Gavin so that they communicated the right things to the business. These were

- *TN2U was about opening up new markets.*
- *The division was going to deliver new growth to the business.*
- *It would provide staff with new opportunities.*
- *It would provide security for the business in the future.*
- *It was building on the company's core strengths but in a new sector.*
- *It was not a threat to the existing B2B offering, it was all incremental.*
- *It was capitalising on the demographic trends towards an older, richer population.*
- *It would increase the profitability of their whole business.*

That was all good, and they had agreed on a standard PowerPoint presentation that could be delivered to all employees. Things had started to go wrong when Gavin had decided that, as it was about personal service, it would be better presented personally by each manager, rather than as a big corporate event. The standard presentation would ensure that the key messages were consistent, but he wanted the individual branches and departments to be able to communicate to their own staff in a way that would be most engaging and motivating.

There hadn't been a unanimously rapturous reception to the launch and Bobbi was worried that maybe the presentations had not been delivered consistently across the business (if it had even been used at all in some areas). Her worst fears had been realised when Colin had cornered her and proceeded to tell her (with some excitement, she thought) how differently and how badly, the message had been received in the different areas.

'Well, as you can imagine,' he'd said, 'in purchasing (with Terry having been relieved of the responsibility for TN2U) he didn't even bother to brief it himself, he let his number two do it. I think the gist of the delivery was 'it's some more fluffy hogwash but as usual, purchasing will find a way to make it work!'

Bobbi couldn't hide her look of horror, which seemed to embolden Colin even more.

'In operations, Phil did his best, but you know how stressed he is. A lot of his team have come to me and said that it seems like a load more work trying to be squeezed out of the same old resources.'

Bobbi let out a sigh, that turned into a groan. 'That wasn't on the brief! How can the message get this distorted?'

'Oh, it gets worse,' gushed Colin. 'In some of the local operational sites, they're talking about balloting for industrial action to protest against job losses due to the "downgrading of the business services division" in terms of status and investment.'

'What?' exclaimed Bobbi 'How many times in the brief did it say it was NEW investment and opportunity? Which part of incremental do they not understand!'

'Hey,' said Colin, shrugging his shoulders with his palms turned upwards, 'don't shoot the messenger, just thought you would like to know.' Was it her imagination or was Colin almost skipping as he walked away?

Now Bobbi sat at her desk and shuddered as she remembered yesterday's encounter with Colin. She focused back on the email she needed to write to Gavin. TN2U needed saving. It needed briefing properly to stop it being over before it began. They had done all the central consistent messaging properly, but the individual approach had led to wild variance in delivery and huge misinterpretations at the employee level. She realised that the fact that Gavin had just sent the presentation to the department heads with a covering email had not helped the situation either. They hadn't heard the presentation delivered enthusiastically themselves and heard the correct context. She needed to come up with some positive ideas to fix this; she couldn't just send a moaning email.

By lunchtime, Bobbi was a little stuck. She had loads of ideas but was struggling to refine and articulate them and wasn't even sure if they were very good ones. She had also wanted to fact check some of the things Colin had told her yesterday – it would be very stupid to suggest there was an issue and come up with solutions only to find out all the gossip was wrong. Unfortunately, she had found out it wasn't wrong. Colin may have exaggerated some of the feelings but the general points that he'd been making were correct. It was time to clear her head – a coffee and sandwich at Black & White seemed a great idea right now.

Bobbi opted for a falafel and quinoa wrap to go with her latte – nothing too heavy. As she sat down, she picked up the latest edition of the newspaper-style updates that came out each month, on the chain in general and Old School Roastery coffee in particular. It was entitled The News in Black & White.

A lot had been happening. Old School Roastery coffee had gone national and was listed for sale in Waitrose. It had also won an award at the Coffee Society's annual bash for best ethical initiative with the single estate coffee from Tanzania, which had already built five schools in the local area. Additionally, the roll of honour of previously excluded kids who were now in full-time employment stood at over 100.

The results were exceptional, and Bobbi could tell that all the staff were buzzing about it. A new lady who served her the coffee had suggested that she read the newspaper and she could hear Gill talking in detail to another customer about the achievements. 'It's so amazing and makes us all feel like we work for a company that's making a real difference to people's lives both at home and abroad,' she enthused.

Bobbi listened with a touch of envy. 'You can't BUY employee engagement like that,' she thought. 'Oh, to have a touch of that in Terra Nova.' Bobbi couldn't help but be intrigued (again) as to how they had executed this communication so well across the business. There were photos of staff from many different branches celebrating in their own way. There was also a link to an online Black & White community where you could post your thoughts and messages. She quickly went to it on her phone and every single comment was good. Being a slight cynic, Bobbi looked for the forum rules at the bottom of the page. A small note said, 'This site is unedited – please keep it clean'. 'Amazing!' she thought to herself. How had they achieved this seemingly united approach from across 50 different sites and the support office teams as well?

She saw Scott and grabbed him. Perhaps she could steal some inspiration for her note to Gavin, she thought. 'How did your business manage to brief all this out so that across 50 sites seemingly everyone has the same message, and you get the same positive response everywhere?' she asked.

Scott looked a bit nonplussed. 'Is that particularly amazing?' he asked.

'You have NO idea,' Bobbi replied. 'Please tell me.'

Scott thought for a bit and then replied, 'I guess, if I think about it, the owner's great skill is making everything appear relaxed and informal, but actually to plan and execute everything meticulously.'

He thought a bit more as if he were discovering how it was done himself for the first time. 'Basically, we bought all the staff in one hour early (paid for) so we could brief everything undisturbed. The managers prepared coffee and breakfast for their teams (having been briefed personally by the owner at the previous week's coffee club meeting). Then we had a simultaneous streaming of a webcast by the owner displayed on our biggest TV over there. Whilst it was on, the staff could grab a central iPad and type in any questions or comments which then came up on the screen and the owner was able to capture them all and answer them at the end. I guess that was clever because everyone got the same information, general questions weren't duplicated and everyone saw the answers to every question, even ones they hadn't thought of, or ones they had thought of but had been too shy to ask. This was followed by two of the previously excluded kids telling their own stories of how the vocational initiative had changed their lives – that was a bit of a tear-jerker, I have to say! Then finally we had a video at the end of one of the schools being built from the funds provided by the single estate coffee in Tanzania – lots of happy schoolkids is also good for stirring the emotions! Then we finished the central section and ensured all questions had been answered. Then we let each local manager talk about the contribution made by the local team and how it had helped.'

'That's great,' said Bobbi. 'So, it was mostly centrally controlled with a bit of local content?'

'Yes, but the company also made a sum of money available for each briefing that the local teams could use to celebrate success in a way they chose amongst themselves. Some of the younger teams just wanted a night out, others wanted a BBQ, others had a family fun day out, while others organised further fundraisers. It was a great message, fun to deliver, and celebrated in a way that, as far as possible, suited all staff. We had a great BBQ here,' Scott ended with a reminiscing smile.

Bobbi (as she was now becoming accustomed to being) was astounded. 'So, you had a strong central message delivered consistently and transparently, which was embedded locally in a meaningful, personal way, and celebrated in a way chosen to best suit each team?'

'You're pretty good at summarising what we do succinctly,' laughed Scott. 'I guess that's pretty much the shorter version of what I was trying to say. I can tell you all the gory details next time we go out.'

'Hmmm, what do you mean "next time"?' Bobbi smiled back.

Bobbi's mind was swimming with ideas and initiatives as she made her way back to the office. Thanks to Black & White she again had some great ideas to share with Terra Nova to do business better

Terra Nova Review

Now review that situation and think about it in the context of your own business or team – what can you learn and apply or change?

Specifically:

- *What are the key differences between the way the two businesses briefed their teams?*

- *What do you think was the most important in the process – the timing, planning, location, etc?*

- *What can you apply to your next piece of communication to make it more effective?*

CHAPTER SUMMARY

Virtually all employees believe that communication has an impact on tasks performed every day. This emphasises the critical importance of communication in today's workplace.

Effective communication is the one thing that you cannot overdo, and an average plan communicated excellently will always outperform an excellent plan communicated poorly.

If you succeed in creating effective communication, it will help your business in terms of speed, consistency, and compliance, and it will also keep your team motivated.

You need to remember that communication is a two-way process, and the effective approach involves asking questions and listening, as well as telling.

Excellent preparation is vital for effective communication. It needs to be the appropriate message, at a time, location and place using a communication method appropriate to your audience. Think about who you're communicating to and ensure that your content, style and timing work best for them, and is not just convenient to you.

Effective communication has a multiplier effect. The better you are at doing it, the better your results will become. Not just in a straight-line trend; good communication can also improve your performance exponentially.

NEXT STEPS

If you have a piece of communication you need to do, you need to consider the content and the method.

In terms of content, consider the following questions:

- What are the three to five key points I want to get across?

- Are they clearly articulated and ideally repeated?

- Do I need to clarify our starting position to avoid confusion and create a common point to begin from?

- Is there any potential confusion over the targets or goals mentioned?

- Can I think of any cynical or sceptical criticism that I can pre-empt?

- What's the right language and positioning to use?

With regards to the method, I again favour a matrix to ensure that I'm covering all the key points regarding the approach. In the example below, I'm briefing different aspects of the business differently and at different times and to a differing extent.

	Time	Location	Length	Feedback
Operations	At the beginning of the shift (paid for their time)	Ideally on the shop floor	10 minutes	Q&A session, capture all questions from different briefs and feedback later
Sales	08h30 before they start their sales calls (paid time)	Sales office	15 minutes	Q&A session, capture all questions from different briefs and feedback later
Office staff	09h00 at the start of their day (paid time)	Office	15 minutes	Q&A session, capture all questions from different briefs and feedback later

Senior management	During the day or at a separate event	Private meeting room or offsite	1 hour	Q&A session, in detail, talking through and discussing any issues that arise. Ensure complete understanding
Total Company	Ongoing	Videos to all staff Posters Screensavers, etc	Ongoing	Ongoing focal point for questions with prompts and email address running along the bottom of the screen

CHAPTER 6

Embed

* * * * *

'Learn from yesterday, live for today, hope for tomorrow.
The important thing is not to stop questioning.'
- Albert Einstein (physicist)

* * * * *

What is it?

To *embed* is defined as 'to fix an object firmly and deeply into a surrounding mass'. In the context of this book and the ideas we're looking at, the 'object' is the vision you're launching or the new project you're trying to develop, and the 'surrounding mass' is the business and its DNA. We want to get to a position where your new vision, mission and values, or your new business initiative, are no longer seen as 'new'. They are no longer seen as an interesting idea or 'the thing that the boss keeps talking about'. They need to be seen as 'the way we do business' or 'the way we do things around here'. Once you've achieved that then you know that the new ideas have been truly embedded into the business and they're secure.

Why is it important?

If you want to progress to new challenges and new opportunities, it's vital that you're able to embed your new vision, mission, values or processes into your daily routines. It's vital that everyone in the business has been engaged and motivated and that they see the new elements that you have introduced, as 'business as usual'.

If these things are not embedded in the business, then they'll decrease and cease. If they're seen to be an 'add on' or a 'nice to have' and have not become part of the company's DNA, then they will fail.

Also, if you're the only one who can evangelise and push the initiatives, then ultimately they will either fail or you will be unable to move onto the next challenge or opportunity. You need to have embedded the initiatives, clarified the vision, galvanised the team, and recruited and nurtured evangelists to do the work for you. You need to have enlarged your actions and communicated again and again to get things visible and committed to by the business. Imagine how difficult it will be for your team if these things are not clear, and if the direction of the business, the processes that are used, and the communication methods are not embedded as standard. It will be confusing and overwhelming for new recruits who know nothing of the history of the business if all these key pillars of your company foundation are still fluid and changing. Finally, you need to embed everything into business-as-usual so that you can be confident that the impact, benefits and direction of travel will continue without you so that you can move on to the next issue.

If you do this well, it's like putting down a layer of sedimentary rock that everything is embedded in and solid. Some of the initial impact may be eroded over time but, fundamentally, the foundation is sturdy and doesn't rely on you to hold it up. You can then move onto the next project. Once that's done effectively and embedded then you'll have deposited another layer of rock. If you do this consistently, you'll end up with a rock-solid business with layers of different value-adding ideas cemented in place and held together by the glue of the values and vision of the business.

It is like the parable of the wise man and the foolish man from the bible. The wise man built his house on the rock and the foolish man built his on the sand. When the rain came down the foolish man's house was washed away but the wise man's house stood firm. If you embed your processes into the business then the business stands on the firm rock-like foundations and will stay strong, even in turbulent times.

Conversely, if you don't do this then you're like the foolish man and the foundations of the business will be like sand. They'll be easy to wash away because you haven't taken the time to embed them in and spread the burden and motivation across the whole business. The danger of not embedding the new ideas and making them rock-like is that your business will be washed away the first time it faces difficulties or a storm.

I want you to visualise this because it's critically important. The vision or initiative is crucial and therefore needs to be embedded deep into the business. It's the foundation that everything is built on, not the pretty roof that you put on top. Roofs may blow away, but foundations stay forever. That's the image you need to think of when you consider how well-embedded the key elements of your business are.

How do I do it?

I think the embedding process is best split into two elements. You can't just instantly deeply root something into the business, and have it work perfectly (well, not very often anyway). The two-stage approach I recommend is to INTEGRATE and OPTIMISE.

Integrate the new initiatives into the fabric of the business. Just get it done; just start. Don't await perfection but concentrate on getting 'good' integrated. Once you have done that, then you can optimise, fine-tune, adjust and perfect. Imagine a marksman shooting at a target. They don't hit the bullseye straight away, but they do take some shots, they do get going. Then over time, they optimise. They allow and adjust for the wind, they adjust the sights on the rifle, until they're hitting the bullseye continually. If they refused to shoot until they were certain of hitting the bullseye, then they would never start shooting. *Integrate and optimise, it's the best way to progress.*

1. Integrate

The key to integrating is to ensure that all things are operating in alignment – the integration of your vision, values and goals in all aspects of the business, however minute.

The story goes that President John F. Kennedy was visiting NASA headquarters for the first time in 1961. While touring the facility, he introduced himself to a janitor who was mopping the floor and asked him what he did at NASA. He answered, 'I'm helping put a man on the moon!' THAT is when you know that your vision is integrated through the business – when everyone knows that the job they're doing is contributing to the overall goals and vision of the business or organisation.

How to integrate

To be an integrated business, and thus to operate with integrity, you need your vision to be in harmony with all of the following areas (and some will require tough choices).

Company values – it may seem obvious, but you need to ensure that your values support your vision, or you're off to a losing start. For example, a travel company whose vision was 'to lead the luxury travel sector in terms of unique experiences' could not really have values of being

- hard-nosed
- cost-conscious
- ruthlessly efficient

Behaviours – management and leadership behaviours should model the values (which should support the vision). If they don't, then customers, employees, and suppliers will pretty soon see through them. If they do, then you generate trust – and trust within an organisation and among stakeholders is a key source of competitive advantage.

TRUST = SPEED

Imagine your boss walks up to you one day and says, 'Hey, could you please get this new product delivered to customer Jones as soon as possible? They've agreed to try them for us, and we're giving them five cases free of charge.' If you trust your boss, you'll just get on with it. If you don't trust your boss, you'll second guess every element of the simple request.

- New product? What product?
- Why customer Jones – what's so special about them?
- They need them as soon as possible – are you sure?
- Free of charge – who agreed to that? Could I get into trouble?

You will probably triple and quadruple check everything and may end up not doing it at all, or doing it late, or giving them just one case.

That's a simple example of greater trust meaning greater speed.

The more your team see your vision and values reflected in your behaviour, then the more they trust you, and the quicker progress happens towards your goal.

Recognition – boy, oh boy, is this important!

If you have visions and values aspiring for one thing, and then reward behaviour that's not aligned to that – then your dreams will be dead in the water. Your credibility will be gone, and your team will be heading out of the door.

'Our values are customer relationships, integrity, and teamwork,' you proclaim. Yet, you promote salespeople who deceive their customers, you reward selfish ambition, and you praise accomplishment above all else.

Either you don't believe in your values (which is a major problem), or your team will never believe in them, or act in accordance with them because your reward and recognition structures are not aligned.

Sometimes you have to go out of your way to recognise something a person has done – which others wouldn't normally do – that really reinforces your values.

For example, this month you announce that the employee of the month is Emma. Let's say that she spotted an invoicing error where you've been overcharging a customer for two years. She brought it to customer's attention and you've credited them with £10,000.

Imagine – £10,000 off the bottom line and she gets rewarded! Yes, because it reinforces your values of customer relationship and integrity. That's such a powerful statement and will embed your values better than multiple presentations.

If in a few months you could then announce an extended contract with that customer on the back of these values, that would just double down on the benefit.

Appraisals – appraisals are another opportunity to reinforce the vision and values into people's actions.

Reviewing the team's behaviour in line with the values and looking at their objectives and achievements as measured against the vision and mission will subliminally (and obviously!) cement the importance of these things in the minds of the team. In Bidfood we seek to define what we expect in different types of job roles in line with the values, in what we call our Value Enablers Matrix (see page 145).

Discipline – this is usually an area where tough decisions need to be made. If an employee is consistently missing targets, and not living the values then that's usually an easy choice in terms of counselling, training, targeting or exiting the business.

If a person is consistently missing targets but absolutely lives and breathes the values, then that's a little trickier. Ultimately though, everyone will also know that he or she is a continual underachiever and so will expect some form of training and sanctioning if performance doesn't improve.

The hardest ones are usually (but shouldn't be) the superstars who completely disregard the company culture and values. They're your top salesperson or most efficient operator, but behave diametrically to your values. What do you do? *You have to tackle the issues.* this is sometimes easier said than done – **but if you put profits or productivity before principles you will never establish the culture and values that you want in the business.**

You obviously try to redeem the situation – counsel the individual, target correct behaviour and so on, but ultimately, you'll be judged by the rest of the team on the way you deal with that person. They will be able to tell if you believe those values or if they're just a nice poster on the wall – and they will act accordingly.

So, the bottom line is that the most important thing is *not* the bottom line. It is your integrity, your principles, your consistency of word and deed, that creates long-term success.

Communications – finally, stitch everything together and align it through clear and consistent communication. Whether it's internal or external communication, take every opportunity to reinforce your vision, mission or values.

As stated in the previous chapter, at Bidfood we try to include values or key ingredients references in every communication and social media post. For example:

As our mission is to make customers' lives easier and help them to grow, at Bidfood we have…

In line with our vision to be the best Food Service Company, Bidfood have recently invested in…

On Twitter or Instagram, we would reinforce our key ingredients to success by tagging every tweet or photo #bestteam, or #forwardthinking, etc.

	care "take pride in what you do, no matter what you do"	**share** "work together to make great things happen"	**dare** "take brave steps to deliver extraordinary results"
CUSTOMER FACING	Customer first, solutions focussed Humility, honesty, integrity Kindness and respect	Builds confidence with customer, great communicator Feedback customer views Works with others to serve customer	Owns problems Passionate about service excellence Looks for ways to work together to improve
OPERATIONAL	Safety first, process focussed Accuracy, consistency, quality Kindness and respect	Communication for smooth running of operation Knows impact of their role on service and works with other departments for excellence	Positively embraces change Keen to learn Looks for ways to work together to improve
BUSINESS SUPPORT	Internal customer first, solutions focussed Humility, honesty, integrity Respect impact on other areas	One team mentality Works with others for service excellence Canvasses and informs stakeholders	Looks outside for best practice Keen to self improve Looks for ways to collaborate on improvement
PEOPLE LEADER	Manage processes consistently Treat all fairly and create a safe environment Recognise team contributions to deliver against the values	Promote knowledge sharing and collaboration Listen, and give honest and constructive feedback Share the vision for success and build trust	Value potential and empower to make decisions Strive for continuous improvement and support people through the changes Embrace self-discovery and independent learning

This constant, and consistent communication internally and externally through all available media will ensure that your vision, mission and values remain front of mind for your team, suppliers and customers. It will give you a clear, stable position in the market – who you are as a company, where you're going, how you're going to get there and how you're going to behave on the way.

2. Optimise

* * * * *

'Optimisation simply means that you take a bunch of little things that don't seem to be very difficult to change and all of those little changes have a multiplying effect – and you get GIANT change from all those tiny changes.'
- Tony Robbins (Motivational Speaker)

* * * * *

Optimal performance means that something is operating or existing at the best level or state it could achieve. Therefore, the process of optimisation is the continual process of tweaking and refining performance in a structured and logical way in an effort to reach that optimal level.

Two important things to note here. Firstly, the process would be continual – certainly, it's not a 'one or two shot' approach. You have to be committed for the long haul, and not be afraid of change.

Secondly, it's done in a structured and logical way. Making continual changes in an unstructured and illogical way is, at best, tinkering, and at worst, sabotaging!

My plan for optimisation looks a bit like a funnel. In the early days, you do probably need to tweak everything you're trying as you won't know at that stage what the winning strategies and actions are, versus the not so effective ones. At this stage, it may look a bit like tinkering as you try difficult adjustments in many areas.

The key to narrowing down the funnel and getting some focus is putting in place, monitoring and being prepared to ACT upon an effective feedback mechanism. (I will cover this in the next section.)

Using this process will allow you to back the winning plan and activities and maximise your effectiveness. The other element to remember about optimisation is that it's also about how you optimise your resources.

Once you've been through the phase of trying everything and optimising everything, then you'll start to see what's working and what isn't; what has some traction and some support, and what doesn't. At this stage, you need to optimise your resources, whether that's timing, money, rewards or incentives, etc. Many companies' first limitation is one of cash flow, so stop spending on everything, and start spending on and prioritising what works.

If you don't optimise, you don't improve. If you don't improve, you die because you'll get overtaken by others. The chapter entitled 'Increase Everything' could also apply here. You need to take massive amounts of action to optimise what works and change what doesn't. You must be continually searching for improvement.

The main reason you'll need to optimise is that you'll hopefully have implemented something that's not perfect. That sounds counter-intuitive. 'Of course, we want to launch something that's perfect,' you say, but the sad fact is that many people and businesses have failed due to the search for perfection BEFORE taking action. That's the key to success or failure. *By all means, seek perfection – but seek it through improvement, not in the planning phase.*

Get going, get started, do something – you can improve it later. You can optimise as you go but if you try and plan your way to perfection you will probably stagnate and die before you get anything launched.

This is so important that it's worth repeating.

The lure of perfection can stifle innovation and create fatal delays.

Whether it's a product, a service, a vision or a new organisational structure, thinking through every iteration, objection, and potential problem and how to deal with it will create a quagmire of doubt and delay.

You'll never guess everything your customers or your team may think, so just get on with it! Don't be rash or reckless. Do be thorough, do test different scenarios but the best feedback is the real feedback of the market. Get your product, service or plan out there. Listen to feedback, optimise and improve.

Apple didn't launch the iPhone X – they went from 1, to 2, to 3 and so on. They won't stop at 10 but they will optimise and improve continually.

Another thing I guarantee is that if you optimise based on feedback, you'll have way more success than trying to launch perfection. If people see improvements and changes as a result of feedback on their comments, they'll be all in! They'll be emotionally invested in the success of that project or service because they were involved and their DNA is present.

Harry S Truman (33rd President of the United States) said, 'There is no limit to what we can achieve as long as we don't mind who takes the credit.'

So, don't hold everything close to your chest to maximise your ego – get it out there! Share, talk, be open to criticism, be open to change – but keep your eye on perfection and optimise your way there.

How to optimise?

To a certain extent, I've covered a lot of this, but it's so important that it is worth revisiting.

Ready, Fire, Aim!

We're always taught, 'Ready, Aim, Fire' but actually, 'Ready, Fire, Aim' is so much more effective in the long run. Get your product, service or plan ready, then fire it out there! Then focus on optimising and aiming towards the target.

You need four things working well for effective optimisation.

1. Openness
2. An effective feedback mechanism
3. No sacred cows
4. No politics

1. Openness

Openness has to come from the top, from the leader. Everyone has to know that you're open to fair questioning and criticism and that you welcome feedback positively.

I remember an old boss of mine – who was a very open man – but was having a hard time convincing us of something that he'd made up his mind on. Most of us were not commenting much because we realised that in this case the decision had already been made. However, one of the younger team members decided to argue the point, possibly because he really cared about this point, or maybe just to raise his profile in the team. The debate went on for five or ten minutes and eventually my boss just shouted, 'Look – you just tell me what you think, and I'll tell you why you're wrong!'

I still remember that line, and as I say the man was very open, but it shows how words last and impressions last longer. Be open and accepting of all points of view. Over time you can be more discerning about who you listen and react to but initially, both for good feedback and to show good intention, be open to all.

2. An effective feedback loop

I won't be too prescriptive here but if you don't have a means of hearing the feedback from a wide range of sources then you won't know what to optimise.

If you're seeking feedback on a product or service, then it can be quite straightforward. You can use aftersales follow-up calls or emails to find out customer response. Customer focus groups could also be done on existing users, non-users and lapsed users to find out the areas to strengthen or the areas to improve.

If you're looking for informal feedback on culture, or a vision, or a communications project to see if it has landed as intended, then the tool we used at Bidfood was 'Listening Groups'. They do exactly as you think – they enable you to engage the business and listen to its employees in an open, non-threatening, non-influenceable way to achieve actionable feedback.

Once you've received feedback, it's always good to sense-check with follow up. Summarise what you think you've been told and play it back to the responders to check it's correct. This will not only stop any misunderstandings but usually lead to additional feedback being given.

Make sure you demonstrate that you action feedback. Kim Scott (ex-Google and Apple senior executive) tells in her book *Radical Candor* of the time she took over a team in Asia for Google. The Asian business culture was very reserved, respectful of authority, and not used to challenging procedures or suggesting new ideas. She asked repeatedly for feedback on how things could be improved and what changes could be made in the business. Month after month she got no comments or ideas and assumed that they weren't interested. Eventually, she got a comment that it would be really nice if they had better quality biscuits in the meeting rooms. 'Seriously!' she thought. 'We're running a multimillion-dollar business and this is the best improvement idea I can get?' But on the principle of acting on feedback, she got better biscuits into the meeting rooms and, more importantly, told everyone that she had done it as a result of their feedback. Subsequently, that unlocked a host of good ideas and improvement suggestions. If she hadn't been patient and persevered, then she wouldn't have been able to receive these ideas. Importantly, if she hadn't acted on the seemingly minor feedback and publicised it then nothing would have happened.

Running a Listening Group

Listening groups are a way to get an understanding of how individuals and departments are feeling and to assess their strengths, traditions and potentials as well as weaknesses and obstacles.

Objective of the listening groups

- To gather information around what makes the people tick.

- To understand how people think or feel about a particular subject or range of subjects

- To gather information to start the planning process for introducing tools and developing managers or to support managers in engaging in a better way.

Areas of discussion

There are no hidden agendas or preconceived ideas of the outcomes. This information will help guide the way we run this department/ business. We would like you to gather information around

- What makes you happy at work

- What makes you frustrated at work

- What makes you enjoy staying at the business

- How do you like to receive messages from the business e.g. letter, conversation with the manager?

Activity

Propose holding between three and five listening groups with between six and ten people at each one. Try to get a good cross-section of people in each group rather than only those most willing to talk. Each session should last between one and two hours.

Questions

1. What are some of the good things about working here?

2. In what areas could we improve?

3. What are some of the things you dislike about working here?

4. What is the best way for us to pass messages onto you? So that you are interested in it and understand it.

5. How do you describe work to your friends?

6. What is the one thing you would improve about the business if you could?

Listening Group Script

Opening:

Hello, my name is ** and I have been asked to come here today to ask you a few questions about working for us. Names are confidential and it will only be the comments that I will report back. We are asking the same five questions across the business to understand your thoughts and beliefs.

We are holding these listening groups across the company as we would really like to understand how you are feeling about the company and how we can improve day to day life for you. We won't be able to fix everything but if we can work on the key areas, we believe it will make a big difference to you.

Ask the questions and facilitate the discussion

Summary

Thank you, I'll now type up my notes to each question and send them into the research team. They will review all the results from across the business and then put together a plan of action. We will keep you informed of progress during the next six months as it will form part of a plan for the business in helping to improve.

When seeking feedback and discussion from your team to assist you in the optimisation process, the next two points are really important.

3. No sacred cows

Nothing is beyond criticism, nothing is beyond rejection, and nothing is beyond improvement.

Don't hold onto your pet projects or ideas and refuse to hear any feedback – if you do, you may fail. Everything is somebody's favourite thing, so if we all did this, we would all get nowhere.

Again, you must lead by example. Take the thing that everyone knows you're most passionate about and interested in and encourage feedback. Show that nothing is off-limits in the pursuit of excellence.

A question I ask from time to time of my team or people I interface with is, 'What could I improve to make your job easier or better?' By which I mean, what can I improve about myself primarily? What can I do more or less of? What can I start or stop doing? What am I missing or misinterpreting?

Be prepared to be open to potential criticism. Be prepared to act on it. If you don't agree with it or feel that the other person doesn't see the whole picture, then GENTLY challenge it, and probe understanding. Don't shut the viewpoint down or get defensive. At the very least, after gently discussing it, suggest that you both go away and consider the situation – and be open to being in the wrong!

Your sacred cow could be an idea, a department, a cultural norm, a business sector, or even a person. You can usually spot a 'sacred cow' by the fact that your business is slowing down, or just slowing down in that area. Possibly you're less nimble, less responsive or customer retention is deteriorating. Perhaps repeat purchasing is less frequent. Alternatively, it may be more subtle clues that you pick up through your people surveys, listening groups or just office chit-chat.

Whatever it is and however you hear about it, don't ignore it! These issues need dealing with, and quickly, to ensure the continued health and success of the business.

4. No politics

Workplace politics can officially be defined as informal or unofficial and sometimes behind the scenes efforts to sell ideas, influence an organisation, increase power or achieve other targeted objects. To you and me it's probably better known as 'backstabbing', 'brown-nosing', lying, cheating, manipulating or misrepresenting someone else's ideas as your own or completely ignoring someone else's ideas for other reasons.

However you define them, the one thing is certain – ***nothing good ever comes out of office politics.***

It's important here to distinguish between office politics or underhand manipulation, versus organisational and influencing skills.

The ability to argue your point of view clearly and persuasively, along with the ability to create a compelling factual or emotional argument are absolutely core life skills.

Similarly, the ability to state a goal, plan a path to that goal, and to organise people and influence bodies of opinion to help you achieve that goal are also vital to most successful ventures.

WYSIWYG (Whizee Wig) – What you see is what you get

When I first started using computers at work for letters and presentations, what was on the screen was not what ended up being printed on the page. (I know I'm showing my age here!)

You typed into the system editor using the system standard typeface and style. You then had to enter special 'non-printing, control codes' (or mark-up codes) to indicate if some text should be in bold or italic or underlined. Thanks to Apple, IBM and Microsoft, the systems were improved to 'What you see is what you get' – or WYSIWYG (Whizzee Wig).Now, what you had on the screen you could edit and format, and that's what would be printed on the paper.

People at work need you to be a Whizzee Wig! The key to long-term success and building a reputation for honesty and integrity is to always act with transparency.

- Be honest about your goal.
- Be open when you're trying to argue your case.
- Answer questions truthfully.
- Treat others as you would want to be treated.

They want to look at how you act, listen to what you say and believe that this is the truth, this is authentic.

If you say one thing and do another or act inconsistently, they can't follow you. You have to be open and transparent in your objectives, actions, results, successes and failures.

It's the same principle as alignment with your values. Don't SAY that you won't stand for office politics and then DO nothing when you see it happening.

Don't SAY you operate a meritocracy and then ACT like a dictator.

Don't SAY you want honest feedback and then penalise people for giving it (or ignore it).

Don't SAY you believe in empowerment and then micromanage your team.

If you're a Whizzee Wig and you create a team of Whizzee Wigs, then life is so much simpler, decisions are made much more quickly, disagreements are had and resolved swiftly, and the business or team is more successful. It has to be led by you – be more Whizzee Wig.

Optimisation is a key step in the process of success and a major part of your progress towards greatness. Optimisation is both a principle and a process. You must feed the process. You must establish the conditions and principles that enable it to happen. Encourage openness, create feedback loops and opportunities, ensure no sacred cows are grazing in the business, and destroy workplace politics through transparency. Optimisation is another way of looking at continuous improvement.

The Japanese term 'Kaizen', meaning continuous improvement, is often used to sum up a philosophy of constantly looking for ways of improving performance. With its heritage in the Japanese automobile industry, a lot of Kaizen or LEAN manufacturing programmes exist in that industry and other manufacturing sectors. They are very data-driven and focused on continual micro improvements to drive overall macro moves in efficiency and productivity.

Most of us don't work in such data-driven environments but the principle of Kaizen still applies. Continually optimising the performance of all functions and all employees – from the cleaner to the CEO – is fundamental to seeing business improvement. Sometimes this will be meteoric, sometimes it will be mediocre, but as long as it's consistent and continual, then there are no limits to the level of greatness that can be achieved.

Terra Nova Business Solutions

Bobbi was raised from her sleep by the shrill alarm clock. As was quite a regular thing nowadays, she rolled over, hit the snooze button, pulled the duvet over her head, and tried to get back to sleep. 'Just a few more minutes,' she thought to herself. She was fed up after another bad night's sleep and needed the rest.

Eventually, she got up and showered, and fixed herself a fresh orange, lemon, and lime juice – 'This should wake me up,' she thought – and it did! Half an hour later she had reached the coffee shop over the road from the office. 'Even this doesn't feel as great as usual,' she said out loud to no-one in particular. She knew why of course. It still served great coffee and amazing food, and the staff were still friendly and customer-focused, but unfortunately, Scott was no longer there. He had been promoted to run the national roll-out of Old School Roastery Coffee. She did still see him

THE WEIGHT OF WORDS

when he was home as they were quite close now, but she missed the day to day banter and discussion, and he was away a lot at the moment with the national brand roll-out.

She was interrupted by Gill. 'Wake up daydreamer! What do you want today, Bobbi?'

'Oh, sorry Gill, I was miles away. I will still stick with the kale and ginger smoothie, please – every little helps!'

She decided to drink in rather than take away. There was no doubt her sharpness and enthusiasm had waned. She didn't mind not being first into the office nowadays, in fact, she didn't even mind being last in!

She snuggled into a corner sofa, looking at the hubbub around her. It almost seemed a separate world as she contemplated the last six months of her time at Terra Nova. She didn't regret writing that note to Gavin with her proposal of relaunching TerraNova2U (TN2U). The launch had been a communications disaster and need redoing, but as usual, it seemed Gavin was gripped with indecision and ended up doing nothing. Even worse, her note had seemed to cast her in the role of 'awkward and disruptive team member' and maybe not a team player! 'It seems no-one can take constructive criticism around here,' she had thought.

Certainly, her star had been on the wane since she'd written that note. She had been unsuccessful in getting the role of running TN2U, which she had really wanted. The role had gone to John, who was quite a bit more experienced and seen as a 'safe pair of hands' (which is no bad thing but not necessarily what you need for an aggressive start-up business). To Bobbi, it felt like her eyes had been opened to the reality of the business. Her previous loyalty and willingness to overlook errors by Gavin and the leadership team had gone. She could now see all the division, the politics, the cowardice and the lack of decision making for what it truly was – weak leadership and bad management.

Bobbi would be leaving Terra Nova, of that there was no doubt, but she didn't know where she was going to yet. Terra Nova had been her dream. It was the company she had longed to work for with its inspirational leader. She was amazed at how the internal reality was so different from the external façade. She wanted to ensure that she didn't make that mistake again!

She finished her smoothie, and the contemplation of her future made her think. 'What the heck! I'm having a flat white, and some bacon and avocado on toast – that seems better than the office drama right now,' she thought. Besides, she wanted some time to process the TN2U update report that had been sent through last night. She'd been side-lined onto different projects since not getting the top job, but she still seemed to receive update reports even though she probably shouldn't! She noted that the worse the news got the later into the night the bulletins seem to come – maybe hoping to be missed by some recipients!

The update seemed to show that the business was stalling. Sales were declining, staff turnover was increasing and customers seemed to be leaving or spending less – basically anything that could go wrong appeared to be. 'Why?' she thought. 'What had happened (or not happened!) to cause these poor results?' She sipped her flat white and contemplated all she had heard and seen in the last six months since she had moved off the business.

Thinking back, she remembered that things had not started brilliantly. Gavin had ignored her proposal to relaunch the TN2U business in a properly aligned and communicated fashion this time. That hadn't been a great sign. The new director in charge, John, couldn't obviously change that view from Gavin even if he wanted to (there was no sign that he did want to!) but to compound matters he'd decided to undertake a 'strategic review' of the TN2U business, just to, as he said, 'Sense check and confirm the strategic direction with the key stakeholders'. Bobbi translated this as double-checking that everyone knew that he was a team player and covering his backside in case things went wrong! Either way, they wasted about two months reviewing the work that had already been done, and to make matters worse, that had been the critical time to get out and get started. In Bobbi's opinion, that would have kept the initial momentum of the launch going. Instead, it was two months of dither and delay and the opportunity for competitors to copy and catch up on their plans. So basically, two months had been wasted with no progress. As the review had confirmed that everything was okay, nothing had changed either.

She crunched absentmindedly on her seeded toast with smashed avocado, crispy bacon, ground black pepper, and a drizzle of chilli oil – 'WOW!' she thought. 'What an amazing flavour hit. Simple stuff, just quality ingredients thoughtfully prepared and well presented. Business is simple if you just do the simple stuff that customers want, well and with passion, and deliver consistently. Why can't we do that at Terra Nova?' she moaned inwardly.

Going back to her internal review of the past few months she recognised that another of the reasons for underperformance could be the misalignment between the company aims and aspirations, and some of the leaders and teams. Take the TN2U cleaning and laundry business, for example, run by Derek. He's a nice guy, she thought, but he was an accountant! Bobbi knew many accountants who were great leaders and inspirations, but they generally had a degree of commercial common sense, and people skills, as well as accountancy skills. Derek was just an accountant focused on the numbers and the bottom line. He was obsessed with the KPI's – what was the average cost per load of washing, and what was the net margin per load, rather than 'How can we grow our sales? Are the customers happy with the proposition? Where else can we add value? What's the customer prepared to pay? What problems do customers have that we can solve?' and so on.

The values and mission of the cleaning business were focused on customer delight but the weekly and monthly recognition awards were given for margin improvement and cost reduction. If you focused on sales growth and customer delight then it was highly unlikely to be recognised as a good job in the short term, even though in the long term it should lead to a more buoyant and prosperous business.

Bobbi tried to stay objective. Yes, she was really annoyed initially after being passed over for the main job, and that had lasted for a few weeks, but now she felt resigned to accepting the situation. She saw the business and the leaders for what they were, and she knew she was going to leave. She decided that she was being objective and would just use the situation to learn what NOT to do in certain situations for future reference.

Too much office politics was another major problem, Bobbi decided. She hated it when people decided to play games instead of just getting on with their jobs, and it had been a particular problem in TN2U. Gavin had 'let it slip' that he was unhappy with the relaunch proposal that Bobbi had sent him, and that it was 'unhelpful'. This meant two things happened as a result. Firstly, Bobbi had been pretty much ignored by anyone who wanted to be in Gavin's good books (she had been able to find out who her real friends were as a result). Secondly, it had meant that whatever had been there before was now, by default, untouchable and perfect as Gavin would seemingly accept no criticism of it, and therefore none was offered. 'It was okay,' Bobbi thought, 'but it was by no means perfect.' Things needed improving, goals and values needed refining, roles and responsibilities needed clarifying – but instead, everything was left just as it was for fear of being 'unhelpful'!

'The sacred cows were alive and well and grazing on the second floor of the Terra Nova building,' Bobbi thought to herself and chuckled.

Bobbi racked her brain to think what else had gone wrong, what else had changed...and then it hit her – nothing! Nothing had changed about the offering since it started. John had decided that focus groups, customer surveys, listening groups and so on were a waste of time and money with a questionable return on investment – so they hadn't done any. They had no real idea which elements of the service the customers loved or loathed, what they would improve, what extra services they wanted, what they thought was overpriced or what they would pay more for, and so on. Subsequently, nothing had changed, and judging by the downward trend on the sales line there was probably more that the customers were unhappy with than they were pleased with.

Bobbi thought about this. The moral of the story seemed to be that if you have a good product, but launch it badly, and then do nothing to refine and improve the offering, then the product or service would fail. She realised she had mixed feelings. She didn't want the service that she had been involved with and her good friends to fail, but she was happy for Gavin, John, and Derek to be taught a simple lesson.

She was just contemplating all these things and what she could learn from them when she heard a friendly voice. 'Shouldn't you be at work, you layabout?'

'Scott!' she cried. 'When did you get back? I thought it was only going to be after a few days.'

'Time off for good behaviour,' he said with a wink, 'and I missed you.' Scott added more seriously.

'And how was the Old School (Roastery) Disco?' Bobbi asked (this is what they had cheesily called their national sales conference).

'It was totally amazing,' enthused Scott. 'I've so much to tell you about. Can you do dinner tonight? I can give you all the juicy details.'

'I can't wait,' said Bobbi, which was true. Her day had suddenly brightened up with Scott's enthusiasm and passion. 'I'll see you at Barney's at 8.'

Bobbi was very excited about the evening. She couldn't wait to see Scott obviously, but also, she felt she needed some of his positivity and enthusiasm about work to rub off on her and help her blue mood and negative mindset.

She thought about the relationship that had developed between her and Scott over the last six months and the major shock of his revelation, which she had now forgiven. He had kept talking about the 'owner' of Black & White, and in fairness, she had never quizzed him further on the owner. Why would a waiter know the owner anyway? It transpired that the owner was his uncle – Uncle Charlie, as he'd told her in that rather sheepish way one evening when they'd been having a drink.

'I haven't been straight with you,' Scott had started, 'and I feel bad. The Black & White shop, now chain, is owned by my uncle Charlie. He is an amazing entrepreneur who actually started Black & White as he wanted fantastic coffee with authentic service, which he couldn't seem to find from the bland global chains. He wasn't expecting it to go so well – I guess other people were looking for the same thing as well!'

Scott had gone on to explain that he'd always been like a son to Charlie and had been coasting along in a management trainee scheme of a global food company. Charlie had offered him the chance to get involved with the business in his typical straight-talking way. 'You've got a great opportunity, Scott,' he'd said. 'If you learn the ropes and prove yourself, then you can grow with the business and progress, but if you're no good, or not committed, or lazy – then you're out!'

Scott had smiled as he'd remembered the offer. 'So, I had to choose between learning and growing in a risky start-up or progressing slowly but safely in a global business. To be honest it was a simple decision. I shared his passion for the idea, and we bounce off each other all the time. I wanted to learn, contribute and make a difference – I was all in! It also helped that his full name is Charlie Black and I'm Scott White,' he'd laughed.

So that was how Scott had started as a server in the shop by the Terra Nova building and had seemed to progress quite quickly. It was partly because he'd been fast-tracked, but also because the business had taken off so quickly.

'Yes, I know I was given a head start.' Scott had looked at his feet and had an embarrassed tone. 'But I earned my way up. We were all new, all hungry to progress, and all excited. If my work ethic and results weren't up to scratch, I knew I would be back looking for a job. Uncle Charlie *has been amazing at setting the vision, mission and values of the business, inspiring and galvanising us into action, creating and developing the team, backing what works, binning what doesn't and constantly communicating with everyone. It's been an amazing journey. I think that the next challenge for us will be to capture and document all the 'stardust and magic' into our normal daily operations, so we can grow constantly and steadily without compromising our standards and values and maintaining the magic of the brand.'*

Bobbi remembered that her anger at not being told the real situation from the beginning had quickly calmed down as he'd spoken with such passion – and also because he'd explained that when he'd first met her, he'd fallen in love but didn't think it would go anywhere, as 'you're out of my league'. Once he'd known that they were getting close and that his dreams may become real, he'd told her everything as he didn't want any secrets between them.

They had had great fun together, talking about life and dreams, as well as work (mostly his work as Bobbi's wasn't much fun – although they did have a laugh about some of the characters and stories). She looked forward to catching up with him that evening at Barney's. It was one of their favourite places – a Texas BBQ and blues bar. It had great food, cool music and amazing staff. She ensured that she booked as it was always busy nowadays.

Later that day, as midnight approached, Bobbi was enjoying a red-hot bath before bedtime – one of her favourite treats. As she soaked in the bubbles, she also had a warm glow from a fantastic evening. Barney's had been as great as ever. The food, music and staff were never disappointing. She smiled as she thought of Scott. It was always as if they were picking up on a continuing conversation, they just got on so well. She thought about all the great things that Scott had told her about life at Black & White. She loved his passion for the business, and it actually made her jealous now, she thought guiltily. When she compared it to her negative feelings about Terra Nova, she longed for some of that positivity. His excitement was the same as how she felt way back on that first day, but his excitement just seemed to grow and intensify whereas hers had shrunk and died. Engaged and motivated employees really ARE the best marketing tool a business can have, she thought to herself.

Guiltily, she envied how smoothly things were going at Black & White. She knew it wasn't easy, and she knew that they'd had problems in the same way as every company does, but they'd progressed in spite of that and had seemed to get stronger and more 'together' as a result. It really was down to the leadership of Scott's uncle Charlie, she thought.

He had set out a clear vision and operated the company on core values. He was true to those values and expected others to be so as well. Everything seemed joined up and working like well-oiled cogs. 'Integrated,' she thought. 'That's the word to describe it.' All the retail and roaster teams are working in alignment with one another, there's great communication and seemingly no secrets and no politics. They have clear goals, they do well for others and well for the business and they know how to have fun! It was definitely a great place to work.

They also got stuff done! Take the example of the Old School Roastery. Launched as a hunch to do good, as well as to be excellent. It had been a great success. It wasn't the slickest brand, and the plan had been hatched around Charlie's kitchen table, but they had just got on with it and had refined it as they'd gone along. They had used no brand consultants or focus groups – just a good idea, hard work, bags of enthusiasm, a willingness to learn, no fear of failure or changing direction AND, she thought with a warm feeling, an amazing project leader in Scott!

As she drifted off to sleep later, Bobbi had three trains of thought entwining in her mind. 'What could happen with Black & White and the Old School Roastery? How successful could it be? What would happen at Terra Nova, where would she go next and what could she do? Finally, what would happen with her and Scott?' She was worried that it all felt so amazing!

Terra Nova Review

Now review that situation and think about it in the context of your own business or team – what can you learn and apply or change?

Specifically:

- *Is TN2U embedded in the wider Terra Nova business?*
- *If not, what are the key reasons?*
- *How would you fix them?*
- *How has Black & White ensured that the Old School Roastery initiative is embedded in the business?*
- *Have you embedded your new initiatives and projects effectively?*
- *What initiatives are not properly embedded in your business?*
- *What can you do TODAY to improve this situation?*

CHAPTER SUMMARY

To embed something into your organisation, you need to do two things. You need to integrate the idea with the rest of the business from top to bottom, and then once you've got started you need to keep optimising the product or service until it's the best it can be – even if this is a never-ending process.

To integrate your vision or product or service, you need complete alignment between it and all elements of the business – the values, the management behaviour, the way that you recognise great performance, appraisals, the disciplinary process, and all your communications. Imagine the comfort of a spine in perfect alignment versus one that's all misaligned. Alignment allows speed and trust to grow, so you just need to operate with consistency, clarity and transparency.

Secondly, once you have got started you need to optimise. This is the principle of Ready, Fire, Aim. Don't let perfection be the obstacle to actually starting something in the first place. Get going and then start improving and optimising. For effective optimisation, you need openness which needs to be led by you. It should encourage feedback and challenge. You also need an effective feedback loop and you need to have a system to gain feedback from all areas of the business in a timely and relevant manner. Finally, you need no sacred cows, everything must be open to challenge and change. Lastly, you must avoid office politics.

Be a Whizzee Wig and optimisation and improvement will be significantly easier.

NEXT STEPS

Embedding an initiative or a new workstream or a new vision into the business is essential to enable you to move onto new opportunities without constantly checking that everything is alright. Integrate and optimise. To check if something has been integrated into the business, use the attached integration model as your guide.

INTEGRATION IN THE BUSINESS

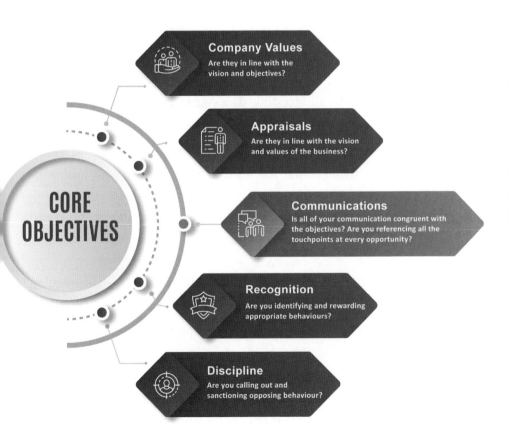

Think of the flow through your business. Envisage how this new initiative touches all parts of the business and ensure that it's congruent and smooth. Identify areas where things don't work smoothly in line with one another and fix them.

In terms of optimising, there's a pre-integration stage and an ongoing stage. The initial stage links back to the chapter 'Increase Everything' where we looked at making sure you back everything completely – ride the waves of success, keep patience with the slow starters and keep up the investment. Obviously, you can't do that forever and, at some point, you need to filter down what you concentrate on. This is the 'optimisation funnel'. After you've increased everything and given all initiatives a fair chance, you need to select what's working. You need to optimise your resource allocation by concentrating on the winners at this point. Utilise all accessible data – customer feedback, employee feedback, financial data, market data, whatever is available. Filter your choices through this funnel and the successes will come out at the bottom, as the winners that you want to integrate into your business.

Once you've done this then you need to ensure that they're integrated as in the attached integration model.

At this point, the second level of optimisation comes in – the ongoing refining of your ideas and initiatives based on sales performance, financial performance, customer and employee feedback, changing competitor behaviour, changing legal constraints and so on.

This is where your constant effective feedback loop needs to be solidly in place and working so that you can continually improve and continually move forwards.

1. PRE-INTEGRATION OPTIMISATION

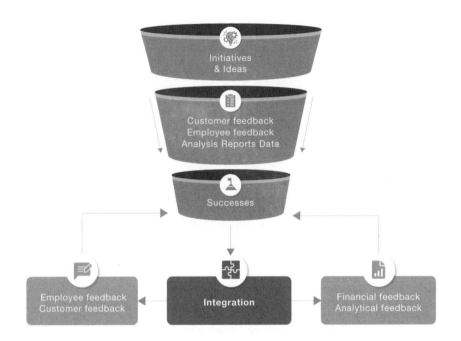

2. ONGOING FEEDBACK OPTIMISATION

CHAPTER 7

Never Stop

* * * * *

*'I don't fear the man who practices 1,000 kicks in a day;
I fear the man who practises one kick for 1,000 days.'*
– Bruce Lee (Martial artist)

* * * * *

'What is to give light, must endure burning.'
– Viktor Frankl ((Holocaust survivor)

* * * * *

*'Nothing in this world can take the place of persistence. Talent will
not; nothing is more common than unsuccessful men with talent.
Genius will not; unrewarded genius is almost a proverb. Education
will not; the world is full of educated derelicts. Persistence and
determination alone are omnipotent'.*
– Calvin Coolidge (30ᵗʰ president of the USA)

* * * * *

There are so many quotations associated with perseverance and persistence. I could have filled the whole chapter with them and each one would teach you something – but you can do your own research!

Management and business are often dressed up as a mystical art. You can do PhD courses in business, you can spend thousands on MBA courses, you can listen to the world's greatest business strategists at expensive conferences. All of these are good things to do and I would never belittle them, but actually, success in business is often simpler…

- Get going, tweak it as you go, keep going!

- Or in other words – **g**alvanise, **o**ptimise, **n**ever stop (but '**g.o.n.**' was never a good title for a book!)

Clearly, there's more to it than that as I've explained in the rest of the book. For example, you need to be clear on where you want to get to and what your goal is before you start on the journey (many people climb the ladder of success to the top only to find they had the ladder leaning up against the wrong wall!).

However, don't get the route planned to perfection before you set off – just get going.

On the way, challenges and opportunities will arise, wrong turns will be taken and unexpected obstacles will appear on your way – just keep optimising.

What is it?

Finally, never stop! You're in this for the long haul. You are pursuing something you believe in passionately, something that adds value and is worth delivering – keep going. Find ways to keep the momentum going forward 24 hours a day, 7 days a week, 52 weeks a year.

Yes – there may be trouble ahead, and you may get negative signals and you may get downhearted – but perseverance can overcome the greatest of obstacles.

Most of us have seen caves with amazing channels and grooves and basins worn into the walls. These have all been achieved over a very long time by consistent drips or flows of water. Persistent water breaks down rock – enough said.

Obviously, you may be getting negative results and pushback because your proposition is wrong or the market has changed, and I will cover this towards the end of the chapter, but if you believe you're still on the right path to delivering something great – never stop!

Why is it important?

It's a bit of an obvious answer – but if you do stop, you won't get to your destination, or you won't get any further down the road to your destination. All of the positive results that you can think of in relation to the world's best companies are as a result of relentless persistence.

Imagine if Apple had launched the iPhone and Steve Jobs had said, 'My work is done here; I can't improve on that product' – they would not now be one of the world's most valuable companies.

The same could be said of Jeff Bezos if he had stopped at selling books on Amazon, instead of extending across numerous other categories.

The best keep going, the best keep growing, the best keep adapting.

So, what are you looking to achieve? What are the results you're looking for with your persistence, why should you never stop?

1. Continued success

Success (whether measured financially or more qualitatively) is the goal of most visions or ventures. Success is not a one-off event. Generally, speaking, we want more success, greater success, more visible success, and ongoing success.

Never stop looking for success. At our business we regularly enter industry awards – partly to raise or maintain our profile, partly to reward outstanding individuals in their areas, but mainly to keep celebrating, to keep proving to ourselves (and our competitors) that we're the benchmark, we're the global standard. Success and celebration are a key part of any team cultures and that's why you should never stop.

2. Continued innovation

If you keep on going, keep pushing the boundaries and keep listening to your customers, you can continue to innovate. Innovation in product, process, service, design, digital media, reporting and so on. Whatever area is important, keep pushing the boundaries.

All around us we see examples of how innovation keeps companies ahead of the pace. We've already considered Apple and Amazon but you can see it in most industries. New developments on a Mercedes S Class or BMW 7 Series become standard on lower models a few years later. The bar is continually raised. A standard Ford or Honda now has as much high-tech equipment as any luxury car would have had 10 years ago.

Customer feedback guides innovation so never stop.

3. Continually changing customer

In most markets the customer wants and needs are continually changing. Sometimes in a huge way, sometimes in small ways, sometimes fast, sometimes slow, but always changing.

You need to never stop listening to your customers, and by that, I mean *really* listening, don't just look for data and feedback that tells you what you want to hear. Don't phrase your feedback questions in a way to get the answers you want.

Ask open questions, look for the 'extra comments', not the 'tick box' answers. Hold focus groups or listening groups with your customers. Follow up personally on customer complaints – is it a one-off or indicative of a system or process issue?

You need to know why your customers are buying from you, why they're not buying from you and why they used to buy from you but don't anymore. Do you still have the same tastes and needs you used to? No, they change. Your customers' needs and wants will change too – you need to decide if you will change with them and broaden your offering, or if not, then how you will recruit new customers to replace the old ones. Either approach is fine – but you need to stay close to your customers to understand the situation.

Similarly, due to changing tastes and needs a customer who previously wasn't your target market may now be in your sweet spot. If you're close to the market, you can sweep them up – if not, you lose.

Never stop knowing your customers and never stop knowing your market.

4. Continually leading

Do you want to lead in your industry or follow? Hopefully, lead! If you're a follower you're never truly in charge of your destiny. You're not shaping the industry but you're following the 'norm' that others are creating for you. Never stop leading your business and never stop leading your industry.

Hopefully, I've spelt out the benefits of leading your business – for you, your colleagues and your stakeholders. But you can never stop! The people you lead, the circumstances you operate in, the message you proclaim, the economy, the competition, the customers and technology – they all will continue to change, and if you don't you will be left behind.

If you think leadership is a 'do once and done' profession, then you will fail. Leadership is a 'get up and do every day' profession – even when you don't want to. If you're galvanising, nurturing, telling and optimising every day, then you will be a leader, but if you aren't you will be losing ground.

Also, you must endeavour to get your company to lead the market. Define the market, don't be directed by it; create it, don't be crushed by it. Stretch your competitors, don't be squashed by them.

In his book, *The 10X Rule,* Grant Cardone talks about DOMINATING in the market, not COMPETING.

That's the approach that will give you the most long-term success. When you dominate you don't worry about the competitors because they're too busy looking at you and playing catch-up to be a threat to you.

When I took over as CEO of Bidfood, we appeared to be too obsessed about what our main competitor was doing – were they poaching staff, doing loss-making deals, doing great promotions or new products? It was talked about all the time. So, for the first two years in that role, I had a rule that we didn't even mention the competition.

Let's get our act together, our vision, mission and values straight, our customer proposition right, our commercials proposals better and so on. In doing so we put clear blue water between us and them – we' aren't dominating the market yet, but the only things that dominate our thoughts are our customers and colleagues.

5. Keeping fresh

Do you prefer fresh milk or sour milk? Fresh fluffy bread or mouldy stale bread? Fresh, vibrant business thinking or mouldy, stale, same-as-before thinking?

Do you decorate your home, change your car, buy new clothes?

I think you get where I'm coming from. We don't like stale; we don't like everything being the same forever – so why would we put up with it in business? Never stop keeping it fresh, never stop keeping it exciting, never stop looking for new ways to motivate your team.

If you want to lead, you must stay fresh and relevant, listening to your customers and adapting your offering. In business as with food – fresh is tasty and exciting. It commands a premium. It's desirable, talked about and – fresh is best! For the sake of your customers, your colleagues, your stakeholders, your sanity, and your bottom line – never stop keeping it fresh.

6. Plugging the leaks

Imagine your business or venture as a nice new wooden bucket. Freshly painted, varnished, and wonderfully watertight. You fill it up with your vision, mission and values and off you go. The bucket is full and engagement is great.

Over time, however, people come and go, the market changes, customers change. The bucket gets bashed about a bit, it gets passed around, tripped over and gradually water splashes out. Small leaks appear in the previously watertight bucket. Before you know it, the bucket is only half full. Your message is only 50 per cent effective, your performance suffers and will do so until you fix the leaks and fill the bucket. Never stop leading, challenging, celebrating and all the other things I've referenced – this keeps filling the bucket.

But you also need to plug the leaks. Maybe you have a department or a manager who is not bought into the vision and is not taking the business in the right direction. This is like a leak in the bucket as all the good work drips away and effectiveness is reduced. Keep reviewing your team, review their effectiveness but most importantly, review their attitude and approach. Ensure they're watertight and engaged in the direction you want to go in.

7. Stoking the fire

Not everyone will share your passion for your vision. Not everyone will feel it as deeply and see it as clearly. Not all your staff are waking every day intent on moving closer to that vision and goal. Their fire dies down and their passion cools. Your job is to keep stoking the fire.

Glowing embers can be brought back to flame with a breath of fresh air and some new kindling. Similarly, your team can be invigorated time and time again by your breathing new life into the vision, reminding, redirecting and re-motivating them in the right direction.

How do I do it

Again, this may seem blindingly obvious – just don't stop! But there are ways to do this that make it more successful.

1. Be consistent

If you have embedded your new ideas into your 'business as usual' processes, then this is a great way to ensure consistency. People often don't like change, especially unwarranted change, so keeping consistent and following the same processes ensures common understanding and improved efficiency. This is not a contradiction to the point on keeping it fresh outlined above. Fresh ideas, initiatives, products and projects are needed to 'never stop' but be consistent insofar as they are aligned with your values and progressing you towards your vision.

2. Be different

In other words, be consistent but also refresh. Acknowledge that all things will not work equally well. When things in a certain area are getting stale or not delivering the results that you wish, then look to do a different thing (or the same thing in a different way). Things could be a new angle or approach in your marketing and communications, a new product extension, an enhanced service offering or a new corporate style to the market. Keeping most things consistent but refreshing elements that aren't performing allows you to keep moving forwards.

3. Keep riding the wave

I talked about riding the wave of success – don't stop! Great surfers ride the waves to the end of the ride, they don't bail out halfway through. In the same way, keep riding your particular success wave and it may even get bigger and crazier. Keep going until the momentum stops, not just until you think you've had enough.

4. Keep publicising

Can you ever publicise yourself too much? Probably, but in reality, the level of awareness that people have of our business, product or service is WAY smaller than we think it is. It's a huge market out there, and the 'noise' of advertising and awareness is continually growing. Grant Cardone (2.8m followers on Instagram) says that he learned to keep publicising his services, even when his friends told him that he was overexposed. His view is that it was only when he started getting complaints from people that he posted too often and in too many ways that he thought he may actually be starting to get through – so he increased what he was doing! This will not work for every situation, but 99 per cent of the time people will not have heard of you, or remember you, or realise what a great offering you have – so keep publicising.

5. Keep rewarding

This ties in with the consistency element. Keep celebrating success, keep rewarding people for doing a great job, but keep doing it in line with the company vision and values. That way you keep people motivated, you ensure that you're consistent, and you reinforce the company vision and values – a win, win, win!

6. Keep reviewing

Are you constantly listening to the feedback from your customers and employees – you should be! Keep reviewing what you're offering against the feedback you're getting. Is everyone still satisfied, or is enthusiasm waning? If so – why? Are the assumptions you made still valid? Has the market changed? Has the competition changed? We have seen many examples of management teams being asleep at the wheel whilst the industry drove past them. Think of Kodak, who invented digital photography but let the market go past them as they didn't want to take the focus off the highly profitable photographic film business. Or remember Blockbuster, who had the opportunity to buy Netflix but missed it and got washed away by the tide of changing customer behaviour with streaming content.

Keep trying to assess your customers' changing needs so you don't get left behind and, hopefully, you'll identify and capitalise on any changes ahead of your competitors. Gut feel is a vastly underused management skill. It doesn't get a lot of attention in books or courses because you can't teach it, but it's amazingly accurate most of the time. Never underestimate the amount of ingrained detailed knowledge and understanding that you have about the market you operate in, as because of that you'll see things and suspect things before others do. Listen to that little voice in your head or that upset in your stomach telling you that something is wrong or that an opportunity exists. Never stop seizing those opportunities and bringing them to market.

Never stop – unless you want it all to end. Whether you have failures and setbacks or successes and accolades, just keep going. That is the most important message about never stopping. Business is an organism, a life form. If you stop, you die. True winners are the people who keep on going, who embrace failure as an opportunity to learn and grow, who keep the end goal in mind and keep pushing towards it. That's what makes them great and successful. Remember that you have never failed until you give up on your goal. All the other setbacks are just learning experiences as long as we keep going. Keep learning, keep changing, keep progressing towards your goal – Never Stop!

* * * * *

'I've missed more than 9,000 shots in my career. I've lost almost 300 games. 26 times I've been trusted to take the game-winning shot and missed. I've failed over, and over, and over again. That's why I succeed.' - Michael Jordan (Basketball legend)

* * * * *

Terra Nova Business Solutions – PostScript

It was an amazing evening! Scott looked dashing in a smart tuxedo and a ruby red bow tie. Bobbi was feeling glamorous in a sequinned ball gown and even Uncle Charlie had scrubbed up nicely. Scott had just picked up an award at the Coffee Industry Awards (or the CIA, as Scott liked to joke!). Old School Roastery had just won the award for Best Ethical Brand at the trademark event. Bobbi was so proud of him and delighted to see him rewarded for all his hard work.

They had been joined at the star-studded night by a number of employees of the retail and roastery operations who had been nominated for recognition by their colleagues. They had enjoyed a fantastic evening with great food, the award obviously and even an appearance by Charlie on the dance floor.

Bobbi was relaxing with Scott and Charlie and having a drink in the cosy bar of the hotel that they were staying in. 'How's the job-hunting going, Bobbi?' Charlie asked. 'It sounds like you made the right move getting out of Terra Nova. My investor friends tell me that there's a disaster waiting to happen in that company.' He pulled his finger menacingly across his throat as he said this.

'Nothing yet,' said Bobbi. 'I'm taking my time to consider what my options are. I want to work in a company that I'm passionate about and to have a role like Scott's. I want to LOVE going to work and be passionately involved in moving the business forwards with like-minded people.'

'You certainly learned how NOT to do things at Terra Nova by the sounds of what you say,' laughed Charlie. They all chuckled and raised their glasses. 'To the reverse training programme of Terra Nova,' declared Bobbi with

a smile. She felt happy with all the weight of the negativity and politics removed from her shoulders.

'So,' said Charlie, suddenly sounding serious, and putting his drink down. 'I want to utilise that very useful training that Terra Nova gave you. We're growing as a business and now have over 1000 employees and growing by 20 per cent a year. What I don't want is to fall into the same traps as Terra Nova and become a bureaucratic and political place to work. I want to embed all of the magic and keep the business growing in the right way, staying true to our values and focused on our customers.

'I'm ready to take a step back and start a new project. I want you to take over running the Black & White retail operation. Scott's doing an amazing job at Old School Roastery and I think that's his strength. I believe that you can take the retail business to the next level. And,' he added with a laugh 'now that you and Scott are engaged, I need to ensure that you get to spend time together.'

Bobbi was shocked but felt no hesitation in her response. Black & White had felt like home from the very first day she went in. She looked at her emerald and diamond ring, she looked at Scott's smiling but questioning face, and she looked at Uncle Charlie. 'YES!' she said without any doubt. 'I'd love to do that.'

What an amazing three years, she thought, and what an exciting next three years and beyond lay ahead. She felt like her life was about to start, her dreams were about to IGNITE!

CHAPTER 8

Using the IGNITE Model
During the COVID-19 Crisis

This model, either in totality or as individual improvement areas, is not just a nice acronym and basic business theory – it works! This chapter shows you how I utilised this model to protect, sustain and transform the Bidfood business during the 2020 coronavirus epidemic. I hope that this will give you a hands-on guide as to how to use some of the principles outlined in the book. As I write this we're still in the midst of the crisis. By the time you read it the crisis may be over but I know that Bidfood will have adapted, developed and thrived.

The coronavirus pandemic has been the biggest societal, economic and business shift in a lifetime. It will undoubtedly have a bigger impact on business and society than the global financial crisis of 2008/9. Coronavirus was officially designated as a pandemic by the World Health Organisation in April 2020, having gone global after its origination in China and affecting nearly 200 countries.

As well as the human cost in lost lives and the health impact, the short- and long-term economic effect of COVID-19 in terms of job losses, GDP decline, business closures and government support packages has, and will continue to be, unprecedented. Estimates of the impact are hard to come by as I write this, as in real terms we're only at 'the end of the beginning' with all countries exiting the first wave of infections and worrying about the second and subsequent waves. Economic forecasters say that the impact on the global economy could be tens of trillions of dollars.

In the UK, the economy and the population were hit hard. The first case of COVID-19 was diagnosed on 29th January 2020, but full lockdown measures were not implemented until March 23rd, 2020. As I write, the UK has the second-highest global death rate of over 40,000 deaths in June 2020.

The impact on the UK economy has been massive, and economists are expecting GDP to be down by close to 10 per cent by the close of 2020. The government introduced the furlough scheme in April 2020 to support businesses to carry on employing and paying people who they may otherwise have laid off due to the impact. By June over 6 million people were registered with the scheme, which is nearly one-third of the total workforce in the country.

In the sectors of the economy that Bidfood supplies (the hospitality sector) many of them shut down completely – restaurants, pubs, hotels, visitor attractions, events, leisure, gyms, etc were forced to close from 23rd March. Whilst we retained some business in care homes, hospitals, prisons and some schools, our overall business in terms of sales declined by 70 per cent in two weeks from mid-March to the end of March.

How did we rise to this unprecedented challenge using the principles of the IGNITE model?

Inspirational Vision

We'd already established our long-term vision, mission and values.

Vision: To be the best food service provider.

Mission: To deliver service excellence, make life easier and help our customers to grow.

Values: Care (take pride in what you do, no matter what you do).

Share (work together to make great things happen).

Dare (take brave steps to deliver extraordinary results).

We believe that inspiring our teams to be the best that they can be, based around living out our values and delivering service excellence to our customers and helping them to grow, is a framework that will deliver continued success. We had also done a 2025 vision based around specific metrics on customer retention, employee engagement and profitability… and then coronavirus happened.

Nothing changes in our vision, mission and values. These should be well-grounded and have longevity whatever the situation. Our 2025 targets looked somewhat out of reach, however! With a 70 per cent decline in business almost overnight we needed a short-term goal for people to buy into. Given the national crisis and the stories of impending doom that seemed to take up most of the news stories every day, that wasn't hard. We needed to SURVIVE in order to THRIVE.

Survival was the message that we preached every day in the first few months. Crucially, the way we communicated this and the narrative that we used was all founded in our core values. This was the time that the strength of the values shone through and reassured me that they were ingrained in the way we do business. Caring for others was critical at this time – colleagues, customers, family members, the ill or self-isolating – this was a key theme running through all our communications and actions. Sharing – working together at this difficult time really pulled existing teams and new teams together, and Daring – looking for new ideas and initiatives to protect and grow the business in the 'new normal' of a pandemic bought some great ideas.

What did we do?

We had several existing, semi-existing and totally new business initiatives that protected our survival. Firstly, we still had a third of our customers trading with us, but their needs had changed. Hospitals and care homes were very busy during this time and often wanted more products from us as other suppliers let them down, especially in the non-food, cleaning and sanitisation ranges. Prisons needed more product ranges as they were providing special gift packs to prisoners to placate them for having visiting rights suspended, and schools that were still open for children of key workers needed more individual 'grab and go' options rather than the usual mass catering products they took. We opened quite a lot of new business in those first few months from operators let down by other suppliers or smaller customers who used to get deliveries from supermarkets that had ceased due to the massive food stockpiling undertaken by many consumers, which limited the supermarket's ability to deliver.

Secondly, we had already started looking at the direct to consumer (D2C) opportunity instead of our usual business to business (B2B) model. We believed there was a desire for larger catering packs and specialist catering products that we could meet, and we had launched a D2C website (catering2you.co.uk) in 2019. Within a few weeks of the consumers stockpiling this website was overrun with demand and we couldn't keep up. We instantly switched our 23 depots around the country to also offer home delivery D2C and 'click & collect' options. We changed our B2B e-commerce site to be a D2C one and set up the logistics in five days. This was a great success and customers loved it. In a month we signed up 60,000 customers.

Finally, we met a national need in co-operation with the government. As part of the lockdown on March 28th, the government identified nearly two million people who were ordered to stay at home completely for three months due to a variety of pre-existing medical conditions that made them extremely vulnerable to COVID-19. A proportion of this population (up to 450,000) was also at risk of not being able to get food as they lived alone and had no family or social support to do their shopping. This was discussed on a government call with industry, with all the major retailers, manufacturers and ourselves present (and also our major competitor, Brakes). The government wanted to create a system whereby they could procure, pack and deliver a weekly food parcel to each of the 450,000 people every week. This was at the time when there were major food shortages, queues and delays in retail while home delivery was almost impossible to get. In a true example of 'Dare' and 'Share' in order to 'Care', we decided to collaborate with Brakes to deliver the solution as we both had 70 per cent idle capacity whilst the retail sector was struggling to cope.

Within seven days we delivered our first food parcels. This sounds so simple, but I cannot overemphasise the herculean efforts of the teams from Bidfood and Brakes to deliver this. To design a nutritionally balanced food box in conjunction with the government, to procure the products at a time of national shortage, to set up picking and packing operations in our depots, and to organise and deliver to people's houses instead of hotels and restaurants, and to get it all going in a week, was simply outstanding.

We were all inspired by the mission of protecting and feeding some of the most vulnerable in society and the feedback we've had continually shows that it wouldn't be an exaggeration to say we were saving lives, as people had no other access to food.

It's fascinating to note the power of an inspirational vision. We compete hard with Brakes every day of the week and have done for years, yet we worked together seamlessly, and with great trust and co-operation because we all bought into the vision of feeding the vulnerable and keeping them safe. That's the power of an inspiring vision. The government described the food delivery program as the biggest domestic relief effort since World War II – and WE were delivering it. That's inspirational!

At some point the hospitality industry would reopen, there would be nervous consumers, worried customers and desperate competitors who had all seen their business decline as we had. Our next challenge was to ensure we were ready for the fight that the next twelve months would bring. I launched a medium-term theme to both inspire and galvanise the team – RELENTLESS! We would have to be relentless to survive, to get the new customers, to see off our competitors and to ensure that we emerged as leaders in the post COVID race. As you know I like an acronym, and the relentless message was condensed as shown here:

R   - RELENTLESS never reckless

E   - Endeavour and discipline. Try new things and stick to the plan.

L   - Leading the industry

E   - Endless energy, for ourselves and our colleagues and customers

N   - New ways of working with ZERO bureaucracy

T   - Total focus on ITEMS and CASH

L   - Looking for new opportunities continually

E   - Excellence in everything

S   - Simplicity in all we do

S   - Shape our own future

It was important in the quickly changing environment that we were in to ensure that the messaging was replaced as needed. Short-term we needed to survive, medium-term we need to be relentless to win in the market, and then, hopefully, we might return to our original 2025 plan. Obviously, a vision would normally be long-term, but this is an interesting case where we used a series of shorter-term objectives to direct and inspire the team (remember, this is real life, not business school!).

Galvanising into action

Bidfood is a great business with proactive people and a 'can do' culture that we've developed over many years. In that sense, the groundwork had already been laid in terms of being able to galvanise the team into action to meet the new challenges of the COVID pandemic in the UK.

I started daily communications with the whole business on what was happening, what the challenges were and how we were, and needed to respond. I will cover that in more detail, but it was a key part of inspiring everyone to rise to the new challenges, especially in the shield pack deliveries (food parcels to the vulnerable people), which were totally new to us.

The communications covered UK news and its impact on us, Bidfood news and what we were doing, and a call to continue the great actions we were taking. When you're delivering such vital services to the vulnerable in the country it's relatively easy to inspire people to achieve great things.

We had twice-daily conference calls with the team delivering the shield packs, to work through issues and keep them motivated. I also had daily conference calls with the leadership team of the company to review how we were doing, ensure cashflow was on track (critical when 70 per cent of your customers have stopped trading) and plan for the future.

I was using all the aspects of galvanising action that I discuss in the chapter – time-related urgency, positive consequences, negative consequences and emotional engagement – all of them were relevant in these unique times. I've shown the letter I used to inform the business about the shield packs on page 199. I utilised our company values as a means to show that despite this being new, it was exactly in line with how we operate as a business.

Nurturing the team

The team I have in place at Bidfood, and that has been developed down through the business, is a great team. They're decentralised, empowered, competent and resilient, so I was not starting from the beginning in terms of nurturing. In fact, the main part of nurturing in the context of this example is safety and anxiety and caring for the team.

Many of the senior management team were under real pressure with the changes that were happening in the marketplace, the changes we were trying to implement in the business and the general anxiety in the country. We were making all the changes we needed to do with the new business initiatives – HR, IT, operations and purchasing all doing things very differently. We had customers who couldn't pay us (or didn't want to because of their own pressures), and suppliers who wanted paying for goods delivered to us but just sitting in our warehouses because of plummeting sales. There were many employees laid off on the government furlough scheme who were anxious about their jobs and the remainder who were working were under pressure and often doing different tasks to normal.

I felt that the main thing I and the senior team could do was to live the values, and especially 'care'.

The main efforts were to protect and communicate. Protect the team members who didn't need to be involved or worry, from many of the pressures being faced. Cashflow and finance were very tight, extra banking facilities needed to be negotiated by the finance team, and debtors and creditors needed chasing up and placating respectively. The contract negotiations with the government for the shield packs were detailed and tedious (and vital). In all those areas we kept the dialogue largely at the senior leadership team level to allow the others to simply get on and deliver to the customers who were still trading and the new consumer customers.

As I said earlier, we had daily telephone conferences with the leadership team, and monthly Zoom calls instead of board meetings. I kept my 1:1 meetings in place and just did them over the phone. There's a danger with a strong resilient team that you assume too much and think they're indestructible. After ten weeks of solid pressure, I knew I needed a day off or two and I also had to instruct a couple of the team members to take a few days off just to recharge.

For the wider team, we had the daily communications and, recognising the unique strains for both those in work and on furlough, we did a lot of support around mental health and anxiety, ensuring everyone could access support if they needed it.

I continued to recognise success, although not with big events and celebrations, obviously! When we had the shield pack contract signed and had been delivering the service for a few weeks I rang each of the people closely involved (about 25 of them) and thanked them all for their efforts and stressed the importance of the initiative to the company. Just taking that structured time to call them all was much appreciated, and I know from second-hand feedback that it made many of them feel fantastic to be told what a great job they had done.

Increase everything

A month or so into the crisis we were trying existing and new initiatives – catering2you.co.uk, home delivery D2C, click & collect D2C, shield pack creation and delivery, opening new customers.

Catering2you and click & collect were not going as well as the other areas, but we continued to persevere and increased our advertising budget on Catering2you and increased our coverage on click & collect. Home delivery was going very well, and we looked at how we could increase that area by improvements to the ordering site, improving the range and doing the necessary legislative changes to allow us to include alcohol on deliveries.

Despite many customers being on skeleton staff, a lot of them were very open to having discussions about giving us their business. They were looking at consolidating supply to one distributor or looking at what savings they could make by changing supplier, or just realising that the lack of business made it an easier time to change their supply chain than when they were busy. We continued to plough time and resources into this area to maximise the amount of new business we would have when the market reopened. We won more new business during lockdown than in the previous twelve months!

On the shield packs we were making nearly 450,000 deliveries a week to people's homes (from a zero base) alongside Brakes, and the numbers were determined via registration on a government website so we couldn't influence the growth ourselves. One evening as I was walking around my neighbourhood, I noticed a lot of houses had put up colourful pictures in the windows, drawn by the kids (who were all at home because schools were closed) thanking all the healthcare workers for their efforts. I had a little 'aha' moment. We were making weekly deliveries to people who because we were delivering, were without much if any social support or interaction. How lonely to be stuck at home for twelve weeks. Despite our deliveries being contactless, we knew that many of the recipients loved a simple hello or quick chat (socially distanced) with our delivery drivers, who were also overwhelmed at the difference it made to the customers. I thought, 'What if we could get the children of our employees (who are at home and probably driving their parents mad by now) to draw pictures and write messages that we could include in the shield packs for delivery and thus brighten up someone's day?' It fitted perfectly with our 'care' and 'share' values as well.

I wrote the following note to all employees at Easter time and also, we created some nice pictures of Bidfood lorries to colour in if people didn't feel too creative. I said:

Daily update
*Wednesday, 8*th *April 2020*

The following brief update is to let you know about our plans and current activity around the coronavirus.

Something to brighten their day – calling all parents!

We'd love to spread some of the joys of spring and help to put a smile on the faces of our vulnerable care-pack recipients. Many of them are lonely, and really miss contact with the outside world, and I'm sure many of you, if you have children at home, are struggling to find things to amuse them. If you have some budding artists at home, or perhaps even a petite-poet, we'd like them to get creative and draw, paint, or write a little pick-me-up for those people who might be feeling lonely while they're self-isolating. Be sure to include a message to let them know who it's from, for an added personal touch.

Whilst general advice suggests that the virus won't live on paper or cardboard for longer than 24-48 hours, it's obviously important to make sure your little ones have clean hands and are working in a clean environment, as the people we will be passing these on to are in the most vulnerable population. Please use your best judgement before passing any artworks to the depot.

Please post or drop-off your creations to your closest depot delivering the care packs (see our Instagram posts for a map), and we will ask the transport teams to hand these out as they make their deliveries.

Fantastic feedback

As we continue to make deliveries to those who need them most across the country, we're receiving some wonderful feedback and thanks. If you hear a story or take some feedback, be sure to pass it on to your depot team. Today I'll leave you with a comment from one of our vulnerable care pack recipients in Manchester:

'Thank you very much for my care package! I want to thank all of you; the drivers, warehouse and all involved at Bidfood for doing an amazing thing to help out at this time.'

Andrew Selley

CEO

Issued: 08.04.20

It was a simple idea that grew and increased the impact of the shield packs immensely. It didn't make us any extra revenue – in fact, it cost us a lot, as we ended up colour copying and printing hundreds of thousands of the drawings, but it made a difference to the lives of the recipients. We got endless feedback like the few shown here, and that makes a massive difference to the motivation of the team and the culture of the business. That's priceless!

Lump in my throat when this came with our shielder food box - thank you Bidfood Staff! 😊

@BidfoodUK **Thank you! Put a smile on our faces!!** 😄
#staysafe #thankyou🙈 #keyworkers

@BidfoodUK This beautiful drawing, from 8 year old ███ made me smile 😊 Thank you so much! It's going straight in my window 🌈❤️

Thank you ███, your picture is beautiful and helped me start my day with a 😊. I hope you, your family and everyone involved in this support is safe + well. You're doing a very kind thing supporting others + making us smile. The future is in good hands @BidfoodUK @DefraGovUK

@BidfoodUK thanks so much for the food parcel you have just delivered from the Coronavirus helpine I imagine? And also if you know who ███████, aged 10 is, please thank her for the lovely drawing that came with it. Made me cry a little bit for the sheer thoughtfulness. Thank you!

@BidfoodUK thank you for your shielding food box for my little girl, this picture inside was such a lovely surprise & has really helped to cheer her up after 9 weeks isolated at home. Please pass on our thanks to you all & the Birmingham team ♥ 🌀 @WalsallCouncil

Tell, Tell, Tell

I've already covered the detail of the daily (or twice daily), weekly and monthly communications we did internally in the business. This was vital to ensuring everyone was in the same place and travelling in the same direction. It was a time of great uncertainty for everyone, and even if the message was not much different each day, it provided reassurance and information. I got a few members of the senior team to share the load and vary the style and that worked well.

With a lot of people on furlough, we faced an additional challenge on communicating as they weren't meant to be accessing company email, and in the case of drivers or warehouse workers, they wouldn't have a company email anyway. So, we launched a company app, especially for staff at home on furlough. A simple and hopefully engaging way to communicate important news, get feedback, create quizzes and surveys and just try to keep all parts of the team engaged. This was an initiative created and delivered by the HR team, a great example of the decentralised and empowered team I am blessed with at Bidfood.

As well as communication internally, we needed a lot of external communications. Social media usage went up significantly as many in the UK seemed to be working from home or were on furlough. We increased our social media communication markedly. The messages were a mixture of

- Bidfood are still open and ready to help you
- Fun and engaging 'foodie' trivia
- Information and guidance for customers over what support was available from the government at this time

- Guidance to help customers thinking of reopening
- Dealing with fantastic feedback (and also queries) on the shield pack deliveries

Our website views were up 220 per cent during this time.

We also needed to do a lot of communication with customers who were struggling to pay and suppliers who wanted paying. Cashflow was critical for this period and the finance, purchasing and sales teams did an amazing job of keeping the communication flowing both ways. It's never the happiest thing to be asking for payment or explaining why payment may be delayed, but you need to be open and clear and consistent, and it certainly worked for us. In many instances, it strengthened customers and suppliers' relationships with us which will benefit us greatly in the future.

Trade press articles, VLOGS, video interviews and TV news interviews were also ways that we communicated and raised our profile. It was a time to be noticed and to be taken seriously. There was so much media noise that we needed to ensure that the worries of the hospitality and distribution sectors were also heard.

Daily and weekly communication are hard, and it's easy to let them slip, but at a time of many mixed messages and fast-changing situations, I believe it really helped Bidfood keep the team engaged and motivated and delivering great service.

Embed

It's quite hard to talk about what we might embed into the ongoing business processes when we're in the midst of the current crisis, but there are definitely two areas that we'll look to integrate, optimise and increase.

Firstly, our social media interaction, which has increased by 14 per cent has reached and touched new audiences in new and innovative ways. We will continue this; we will improve it and we will grow it. This crisis has simply accelerated what was a natural progression anyway and we will embrace the 'COVID acceleration' and run with it.

Direct-to-consumer business. I'm convinced that there is a niche in this market that we can exploit. We will not compete with the retailers on home delivery of full grocery shops, but there is a market there for people who want access to catering pack sizes, or the unique types of products used by chefs. There has been an increase in home cooking and baking (which could be detrimental to the eating out market) so we will exploit our strengths in pricing, range and delivery service to maximise this market in the future. We have started via necessity, and now we will integrate and optimise the technology and product offering to succeed in the future

Summary

I hope that this has given you an insight into how I've used the principles in this book in real life. During the biggest crisis to hit the world economy, the principles of IGNITE have proved to be valuable and profitable. They work in a crisis; they will work in good times as well. I wish you every success.

Further Information

I hope you found this book insightful and inspirational. Please feel free to follow up with your thoughts, questions and comments to me at andrew@igniteyourbusiness.biz

For more resources and reading, please visit my website at www.igniteyourbusiness.biz